POST–TRAUMATIC STRESS DISORDER AND TRAUMATIC BRAIN INJURY—CLINICAL AND RESEARCH PROGRAM ASSESSMENT

HEARING

BEFORE THE

SUBCOMMITTEE ON MILITARY PERSONNEL

OF THE

COMMITTEE ON ARMED SERVICES
HOUSE OF REPRESENTATIVES

ONE HUNDRED FIFTEENTH CONGRESS

FIRST SESSION

HEARING HELD
APRIL 27, 2017

U.S. GOVERNMENT PUBLISHING OFFICE

25–825   WASHINGTON : 2017

For sale by the Superintendent of Documents, U.S. Government Publishing Office
Internet: bookstore.gpo.gov   Phone: toll free (866) 512–1800; DC area (202) 512–1800
Fax: (202) 512–2104   Mail: Stop IDCC, Washington, DC 20402–0001

SUBCOMMITTEE ON MILITARY PERSONNEL

MIKE COFFMAN, Colorado, *Chairman*

WALTER B. JONES, North Carolina
BRAD R. WENSTRUP, Ohio, *Vice Chair*
STEVE RUSSELL, Oklahoma
DON BACON, Nebraska
MARTHA McSALLY, Arizona
RALPH LEE ABRAHAM, Louisiana
TRENT KELLY, Mississippi

JACKIE SPEIER, California
ROBERT A. BRADY, Pennsylvania
NIKI TSONGAS, Massachusetts
RUBEN GALLEGO, Arizona
CAROL SHEA-PORTER, New Hampshire
JACKY ROSEN, Nevada

TOM HAWLEY, *Professional Staff Member*
CRAIG GREENE, *Professional Staff Member*
DANIELLE STEITZ, *Clerk*

CONTENTS

Page

STATEMENTS PRESENTED BY MEMBERS OF CONGRESS

WITNESSES

APPENDIX

POST–TRAUMATIC STRESS DISORDER AND TRAUMATIC BRAIN INJURY—CLINICAL AND RESEARCH PROGRAM ASSESSMENT

HOUSE OF REPRESENTATIVES,
COMMITTEE ON ARMED SERVICES,
SUBCOMMITTEE ON MILITARY PERSONNEL,
Washington, DC, Thursday, April 27, 2017.

The subcommittee met, pursuant to call, at 2:29 p.m., in room 2118, Rayburn House Office Building, Hon. Mike Coffman (chairman of the subcommittee) presiding.

OPENING STATEMENT OF HON. MIKE COFFMAN, A REPRESENTATIVE FROM COLORADO, CHAIRMAN, SUBCOMMITTEE ON MILITARY PERSONNEL

Mr. COFFMAN. The hearing is now called to order.

Good afternoon, and welcome.

Today, the subcommittee will hear from the Department of Defense [DOD] and the military departments on their efforts to address the effects of post-traumatic stress disorder [PTSD] and traumatic brain injury [TBI] on our service members.

For far too long, the real and proven effects of PTSD and TBI largely were ignored. Even worse, service members who demonstrated symptoms of PTSD were sometimes deemed weak or mentally unstable. Thankfully, we know better today and are taking aggressive steps to help those who have endured traumatic stress.

As a nation, we have endured an extraordinarily long period of conflict with thousands of American troops deployed in harm's way. Some, as a result of their combat experiences, suffer from post-traumatic stress or TBI. But PTSD and TBI are not limited to combat injuries. PTSD can arise from any traumatic event, such as sexual assault. We expect the Department to treat all those suffering from PTSD and TBI equally, providing the best appropriate care for each.

For more than a decade, Congress has provided funding and legislative direction for the Department's PTSD and TBI research and clinical approaches. In fact, relevant provisions of law are found in each of the last four NDAAs [National Defense Authorization Acts].

Today, our intent is to review our progress and determine where we need to go from here. Our witnesses are experts in the fields of mental health, and I look forward to hearing their views of our clinical and research progress. If they have any suggestions for the subcommittee, I welcome them.

Before I introduce the witnesses, I would like to turn to Ranking Member Speier for any opening comments she would like to make.

[The prepared statement of Mr. Coffman can be found in the Appendix on page 27.]

STATEMENT OF HON. JACKIE SPEIER, A REPRESENTATIVE FROM CALIFORNIA, RANKING MEMBER, SUBCOMMITTEE ON MILITARY PERSONNEL

Ms. SPEIER. Thank you, Mr. Chairman. Let me join you in welcoming our witnesses here today.

As post-traumatic stress disorder and traumatic brain injury began to emerge as prominent injuries from the conflict in Afghanistan and Iraq, and stories of service members facing difficulty in obtaining appropriate care became more frequent, Congress began to push the Department of Defense to be more and more proactive and increased resources for mental health prevention, treatment, and research.

Since 2004, when Congress first directed the Secretary of Defense to conduct a study of the mental health services available to service members at the time, Congress has provided more than $1.5 billion in funding for PTSD- and TBI-related research. Of this, more than $800 million has gone to over 400 research projects related to psychological health of service members, including PTSD, suicide prevention, military substance abuse, resilience, prevention of violence within the military, and family-related research.

We need to better understand how that money has been used; what, if any, results have come from that research; where are there potential breakthroughs, and what areas may not be as productive; what gaps may exist that should be addressed; and how should we begin to prioritize the demands that continue to grow in this area.

One area that I believe requires more focus is the relationship between TBI and the development of chronic traumatic encephalopathy, an issue that has been getting a lot of attention in particular because of professional football. I look forward to hearing how the Department is taking a leadership role in researching this connection.

Just as important as research is the care and treatment of service members. We continually hear about access challenges and the lack of available care providers. A huge concern to me is the stigma that persists among service members that leads to them not seeking care in the first place.

As we heard at the subcommittee hearing on review board agencies earlier this year, the stigma can lead not just to long-term mental and physical health problems but also employment or financial difficulties, as discharge status may not take into account a service member's PTSD or TBI history, even with liberal consideration guidance.

I would like to learn more about what the services are doing to address these challenges, and I look forward to hearing your testimony today.

Thank you, Mr. Chairman.

Mr. COFFMAN. Thank you, Ms. Speier.

I ask unanimous consent that non-subcommittee members be allowed to participate in today's hearing after all subcommittee members have had an opportunity to ask questions. Is there objection?

Seeing none, without objection, non-subcommittee members will be recognized at the appropriate time for 5 minutes.

We will give each witness the opportunity to present testimony, and each member will have an opportunity to question the witnesses for 5 minutes. We would also respectfully remind the witnesses to summarize, to the greatest extent possible, the high points of your written testimony in 5 minutes or less. Your written comments and statements will be made part of the hearing record.

Let me welcome our panel. Our witnesses are mental health experts for the Department of Defense and the military services and are intimately involved in these issues across their respective organizations and the Department of Defense.

They are: Captain Mike Colston, United States Navy, Director, Defense Centers of Excellence for Psychological Health and Traumatic Brain Injury; Colonel Steven Pflanz, United States Air Force, Deputy Director of Psychological Health, Office of the Air Force Surgeon General; Lieutenant Colonel Chris Ivany, United States Army, Chief, Behavioral Health Division, Office of the Army Surgeon General; Captain Thomas Johnson, United States Navy, Site Director, Intrepid Spirit Concussion Recovery Center, Camp Lejeune, North Carolina.

With that, Captain Colston, you are recognized for 5 minutes.

STATEMENT OF CAPT MIKE COLSTON, M.D., USN, DIRECTOR, DEFENSE CENTERS OF EXCELLENCE FOR PSYCHOLOGICAL HEALTH AND TRAUMATIC BRAIN INJURY, U.S. DEPARTMENT OF DEFENSE

Captain COLSTON. Chairman Coffman, Ranking Member Speier, members of the subcommittee, thank you for your support of our Nation's service members, veterans, and their families.

I am pleased to share DOD's efforts in research and program assessment for PTSD, TBI, and related conditions. Last year, about a quarter of service members were seen for PTSD, TBI, or a mental health condition. Allow me to describe our progress.

First and foremost, we made PTSD and TBI leadership issues, with an emphasis on prevention. PTSD incidents decreased from 17,000 to 14,000 from 2012 to 2015, and TBI incidents decreased from 31,000 to 23,000 over the period.

With regard to mental health across the board, we expanded access to care by tripling our mental health infrastructure since 2001. A recent RAND study validated DOD's progress, finding that DOD outperforms civilian health systems in outpatient follow-up after psychiatric inpatient care for PTSD or depression.

One of our largest tasks is better understanding why PTSD and TBI often present with depression, chronic pain, substance use disorders, and suicide risk. Longitudinal research efforts, such as the 15-year study on TBI, aid our understanding and provide a framework for creating effective rehabilitation and support programs.

Advances from medical research accrue slowly in PTSD and TBI. On balance, it takes 15 years or more to take a medical discovery into clinical practice. Fortunately, with Congress' support, my office, the Defense Centers of Excellence for Psychological Health and TBI, has developed a knowledge translation process for use in DOD. This capacity gives us a pathway for advances in PTSD and

TBI and comorbid conditions so that we can get them to clinics quickly and cost-effectively.

I would like to touch upon program assessment. We have evaluated over 150 mental health, TBI, substance use, and suicide prevention programs over the last 5 fiscal years. This program evaluation has been invaluable. Publication of this 5-year study will be completed later this fiscal year and will help us progress on the vital work of ensuring our funding is tied to programs that work, such as the U.S. Army's embedded behavioral health program and its associated Behavioral Health Data Portal.

I would like to briefly discuss the public health success in DOD that no doubt accrued from our increase in infrastructure, from which we might draw lessons for our Nation in addressing a disturbing national trend.

In 2015, there were over 52,000 overdose deaths in America. Opiate overdose death rate went up to 10.4 per 100,000 in 2015. The DOD rate was 2.7 per 100,000, about one-fourth of that. How was this accomplished? In short, through leaders' focus on the wellbeing of service members and a focused, outcome-based effort on prevention—primary prevention, selected prevention, and indicated prevention—drug testing, provider training, pharmacy protections, and medication therapies.

We hope to generalize some of the successes we have seen in PTSD and TBI incidents and opiate overdose deaths into other public health areas, such as suicide prevention and alcohol use disorders. With your continued support, I am confident that our research discoveries, clinical innovations, and relentless focus on readiness for PTSD and TBI will bear fruit in years ahead.

I look forward to answering your questions.

[The prepared statement of Captain Colston can be found in the Appendix on page 28.]

Mr. COFFMAN. Colonel Pflanz, you are now recognized for 5 minutes.

STATEMENT OF COL STEVEN E. PFLANZ, USAF, DEPUTY DIRECTOR OF PSYCHOLOGICAL HEALTH, UNITED STATES AIR FORCE MEDICAL SUPPORT AGENCY

Colonel PFLANZ. Chairman Coffman, Ranking Member Speier, distinguished members of the committee, thank you for the opportunity to speak to you today about post-traumatic stress disorder and traumatic brain injury in the military and the ongoing leadership you have provided to the services regarding military mental health.

The last decade has seen powerful advances in our understanding of evidence-based treatments for PTSD and TBI. I vividly recall standing outside the Air National Guard headquarters building in Cheyenne, Wyoming, on a crisp autumn evening in the fall of 2010. I had just completed my training in prolonged exposure therapy for PTSD. Thrilled with the excitement about the promise of this treatment, I literally said to myself in the parking lot, "I feel like I have been given the cure to cancer." Growing up, there was no higher aspiration for medicine than that. That sentiment was not entirely hyperbole. Research has proven the tremendous efficacy of these therapies.

Roughly 1 year later, in Afghanistan, I had the opportunity to serve combat warriors coming off the battlefields. There, I understood the importance of having real answers for difficult problems, of greeting elite professionals with elite care.

I have repeated this story many times over the years because it is so important to have effective therapies to offer our patients, who have given so much in the service of our country.

Today, all Air Force mental health providers routinely receive training in one or more of the several evidence-based therapies for PTSD, and all airmen can be confident that they will receive state-of-the-art treatment when they enter an Air Force mental health clinic.

Fortunately, PTSD and TBI rates remain low amongst airmen. Even so, we are excited about the successful translation of research into clinical practice, including requiring evidence-based therapies for PTSD, event-driven protocols for recognizing TBI, and the use of progressive return to activity in the management of concussion.

Integrating behavioral health care into primary care clinics, embedding mental health professionals into operational units within highly stressed career fields, and comprehensive screening for PTSD and TBI following deployments and throughout an airman's career are three additional developments that help us successfully identify and manage these conditions.

On the horizon, the Invisible Wounds Clinic being established at Eglin Air Force Base in 2018 will be a powerful enhancement of our treatments for PTSD and TBI, both as a referral center and as a projection of treatment and expertise Air Force-wide.

Likewise, research partners are helping us evaluate options to repackage the essential elements of evidence-based therapies for PTSD to fit existing delivery systems without losing efficacy. These emerging opportunities are every bit as exciting as the research already translated into practice.

To be certain, there is much work still to be done. The Air Force partners with its fellow services and civilian academic institutions to constantly push the envelope of science so that our treatment techniques and systems delivery grow ever more efficacious.

At the same time, we are studying our systems of care to close gaps in services. Currently, a multidisciplinary task force is identifying and resolving gaps in the continuum of care and the Integrated [Disability] Evaluation System for airmen suffering from invisible wounds, with work underway on 27 specific solutions, ranging from education and training to culture and policy. These solutions will translate directly into improvements in services for these airmen.

I wish to thank the committee for its interest in this topic and for your dedicated support of the men and women in the armed services. I am grateful for the opportunity to appear before you on this matter of importance.

[The prepared statement of Colonel Pflanz can be found in the Appendix on page 40.]

Mr. COFFMAN. Lieutenant Colonel Ivany, you are recognized for 5 minutes.

STATEMENT OF LTC CHRISTOPHER G. IVANY, USA, CHIEF, BEHAVIORAL HEALTH DIVISION, HQDA, OFFICE OF THE SURGEON GENERAL, UNITED STATES ARMY

Colonel IVANY. Chairman Coffman, Ranking Member Speier, and distinguished members of the subcommittee, thank you for this opportunity to provide the Army perspective on providing behavioral health and traumatic brain injury care to our soldiers and their families.

Health care is essential to readiness, which is the Army's number-one priority. I know of no area of health care that has faced as many challenges, made as many changes, and has achieved as many advancements as in Army behavioral health care.

Over the course of my career, I have personally witnessed the impact of behavioral health support for soldiers in countless situations. From small outposts across Baghdad to clinics and hospitals across this country, Army physicians, psychologists, clinical social workers, nurses, and technicians have helped soldiers deal with the consequences of combat.

Just as importantly, I have seen healthcare providers supporting the families of those that have volunteered to serve this country, as Army spouses and children also confront and overcome mental illness.

The history of Army behavioral health care has included many challenges. Early in the wars in Iran and Afghanistan, the Army realized that the size and the organization of its behavioral health force was insufficient to meet the needs of our beneficiaries. In response, it greatly increased resources and expanded the number of clinical programs to serve this population.

Senior Army medical leaders also made a pivotal decision to centralize the oversight and direction of all clinical programs and constructed a small team of professionals within the Office of the Surgeon General to do so. That team set out to analyze the effectiveness of all clinical programs, identify the best practices, and replicate them across the force.

Out of this process came many programs, like embedded behavioral health, which has reduced many barriers to care for soldiers in combat units and improved access and readiness. The embedded model places professionals in small clinics in close proximity to where soldiers live and work. Today, over 450 providers in 62 embedded behavioral health teams support every operational unit in the Army. Data has clearly shown that soldiers are receiving care earlier and needing less hospitalization to receive treatment.

Other innovations were drawn from the civilian sector. For example, school behavioral health had shown clear promise in several school districts across the country. The Army embraced this approach and placed providers directly in schools on Army posts all over the world. Children in 60 schools on Army installations can now see a provider by simply walking down the hall from their classroom.

In traumatic brain injury care, in partnership with the DOD and other services, the Army has implemented a clear set of clinical standards and delivers them in interdisciplinary clinics across the force. Clinicians have reduced unnecessary variance, a key step in improving quality of care. Simultaneously, the Army Medical Research and Materiel Command is advancing its state of the science through a gap-driven research portfolio.

Finally, the Army recognized the need to accurately understand the true effect of each patient's treatment. It developed an automated process to measure from the patient's perspective how symptoms responded to the care. The Behavioral Health Data Portal is now in use in every Army behavioral health clinic and has been used over 2 million times. To my knowledge, it is the most widely used clinical outcome system for mental health care in the country. Soldiers with behavioral health conditions get better faster because of this technology.

This transformation has been possible because the Department of Defense delivers the vast majority of the care for our soldiers with mental health conditions and a history of TBI. The civilian sector could not have adapted as rapidly or as completely to meet the challenges faced by soldiers and their families. As the Military Health System evolves to best care for its beneficiaries, it is vital that we continue to deliver the large majority of mental health care.

While much has been done, many challenges still remain. Like the rest of the Nation, we continue to fight against stigma to seeking mental health care, we search for better ways to keep more soldiers engaged in care until they achieve a full clinical response, and we strive to find new technologies to assist our clinicians in delivering cutting-edge treatments.

I am committed to ensuring we overcome these and other challenges to improve the health and readiness of the force. I look forward to working with Congress in this endeavor. I want to thank my partners in the DOD, my colleagues here on this panel, and you for your continued support.

Thank you.

[The prepared statement of Colonel Ivany can be found in the Appendix on page 49.]

Mr. COFFMAN. And, Captain Johnson, you are now recognized for 5 minutes.

STATEMENT OF CAPT THOMAS M. JOHNSON, M.D., USN, SITE DIRECTOR, INTREPID SPIRIT CONCUSSION RECOVERY CENTER, NAVAL HOSPITAL CAMP LEJEUNE

Captain JOHNSON. Chairman Coffman, Ranking Member Speier, distinguished members of the subcommittee, thank you for providing me with the opportunity to share my perspectives as the director of the Intrepid Spirit Concussion Recovery Clinic at Naval Hospital Camp Lejeune.

Marine Corps Base Camp Lejeune and the surrounding area are home to approximately 50,000 warfighters and their families.

Traumatic brain injury, or TBI, has been described as the signature injury of the wars of Afghanistan and Iraq. Approximately 80 percent of all TBIs are classified as mild. Individuals who have sustained a mild TBI may only experience subtle changes in mood, memory, sleep, and balance. They have no visible signs of their injury but are often struggling to function at work, at home, and in the community.

I remember vividly when I met with a Marine sergeant and his wife in the clinic. I asked him about his medical issues. He told me that all he wanted me to do was fix his headaches so he could get back to his unit and deploy back to Iraq.

I then asked his wife, "What was bothering you?" And there was this dramatic pause, and she burst into tears. And she told me that she felt that she hardly knew her husband since he had returned back from his last deployment, in which he had sustained a TBI. Tragically, the war does not end for those families when the service member comes home. It goes on and on every day, as they struggle heroically to overcome the trauma of war.

The reality is that there is currently no diagnostic tool that is sensitive and specific for mild TBI. However, we have worked to overcome this by developing a holistic, integrated, interdisciplinary treatment model that employs a standard evaluation that includes physical, psychological, and spiritual dimensions. We then use this information to diagnose and treat each of our patients.

We treat these service members like warrior athletes and employ both traditional therapies as well as complementary and integrative medicine to return them to the highest level of function possible after their injuries. We use a minimal amount of medication, almost no narcotics. And over 90 percent of them return to full duty upon completing our program.

The great sacrifices made by warfighters and their families compel us to do everything in our power to support them on their road to recovery. Research in the prevention, diagnosis, and treatment of TBI is one way to fulfill this great obligation. The Military Health System, in partnership with civilian academic institutions, has a robust research portfolio to address gaps in knowledge and improve care for service members with TBI.

For example, we have developed a progressive return-to-activity protocol that give providers guidelines on how to gradually increase activity in individuals in a way that maximizes recovery.

We are committed to caring for people like the retired combat-decorated master chief petty officer who was a patient at Intrepid Spirit. He had been exposed to literally hundreds, if not thousands, of blasts during his career. After he retired, he noticed an insidious decline in his cognitive function, to the point where remembering where he was going when driving and then even driving itself became difficult for him. After an extensive workup in our clinic, it became apparent that he had a brain injury.

To this point, the DOD has an ongoing longitudinal study on traumatic brain injury incurred by members of the Armed Forces in order to better understand what happens to individuals like the master chief so they get the treatment they need.

Because Intrepid Spirit Camp Lejeune is located where the service members live and work, we are uniquely suited to support these important efforts. Every day, as we work with service members—sailors, marines, soldiers, airmen, and coastguardsmen—who have sustained a TBI, we are reminded of the urgency and importance of our mission.

On behalf of the staff at Naval Hospital Camp Lejeune and service members like the Marine sergeant and the master chief that I mentioned earlier, we are grateful to the committee for your strong support. Navy Medicine is privileged to work hard at something that is so important and so rewarding.

I look forward to your questions.

[The prepared statement of Captain Johnson can be found in the Appendix on page 56.]

Mr. COFFMAN. Thank you, Captain Johnson.

Captain Colston, I think you had mentioned that, on TBI, on numbers, that I think that you dropped from 31,000 to 23,000. In what period of time was that? I am sorry.

Captain COLSTON. Between 2012 to 2015.

Mr. COFFMAN. Okay. And so I suspect that this was enhanced safety, because, I mean, TBI is produced by trauma. So how would you——

Captain COLSTON. I think a couple things. I think the OPTEMPO [operational tempo] was pretty similar over those periods. So I know that there is a lot of leader intervention in regard to TBI and in regard to efforts that leaders make to tell people not to get TBIs—safety, other issues along those lines.

As you know, sir, there are very few TBIs on the battlefield right now, something on the order of about 200. MVAs [motor vehicle accidents], sports accidents, and the like are where we are getting a lot of those, and prevention measures can be used in that regard.

Mr. COFFMAN. Okay. Thank you.

A question for all of you, each one of you individually. So I have a concern that a soldier, marine, airman, or sailor might be reluctant on Active Duty to go see a mental health professional or go see a neurologist about the consequences of a TBI for fear of what that may do to their career.

I was a junior officer during peacetime, but I can remember deploying as a rifle platoon commander in the Marine Corps and then coming back. And if I look at the Marines, particularly during the height of Iraq and Afghanistan, that person in that same position that would have been in combat coming back and then, as a first lieutenant then, saying, "Oh, I want to see a mental health professional because I am concerned about post-traumatic stress," and what the reaction for that command would have been; it wouldn't have been positive.

And so I want you to—and I was aboard a ship not that long ago, an aircraft carrier in the Persian Gulf, and ran into the chaplain. And the chaplain was informing me, the ship's chaplain, that he would see a lot of the sailors that would prefer to see him versus see a mental health professional because there was no entry in their healthcare books, in the health record books.

And so if each one of you can comment to me how significant this issue is today and what your branch of service is doing in response to it, to gain access for these military personnel.

Captain Colston.

Captain COLSTON. Yes, sir. Stigma is a huge issue. We suspect that perhaps even half of people who have a condition don't come see us because of stigma. Some of it has to do with security background questionnaires, and certainly we have worked over the last number of years to allay that concern in folks.

One of the things that I remember from when I deployed as an Army psychiatrist was you have to work with the chaplains. In essence, there needs to be a close relationship in a deployed setting between mental health providers and chaplains.

There is a presumption of nondisclosure in mental health. I would never, as a mental health provider, run to a commanding officer with things that don't have to do with the soldier's readiness. I have never shared personal details about patients, recognizing that I need to make it as easy as possible. It is also DOD policy that there is a presumption of nondisclosure, and that policy speaks directly to commanding officers.

It is obviously a leadership issue, and it is one that we need to address closely. And, obviously, GAO has looked at it over a number of years.

Mr. COFFMAN. Colonel Pflanz.

Colonel PFLANZ. Sir, I think all the services are moving to increasingly embed mental health resources closer to the soldiers, sailors, marines, and airmen. We are certainly doing that in the Air Force with our RPA [remotely piloted aircraft] community and our special operators, special tactics, and we are increasingly beginning to take that to maintainers on the units.

You know, this proximity breeds familiarity, and with familiarity there is comfort. And as you get comfortable with individuals, you are willing to come and get care and get help. So the greater we bring care to them, the more likely it is we are going to break down those barriers and their reluctance to seek care.

Mr. COFFMAN. Lieutenant Colonel Ivany.

Colonel IVANY. Sir, I certainly agree with the previous two panelists here. This has been a key focus within the Army. I think we have made quite a bit of progress in this area.

If you compare the number of mental health visits that were delivered in 2007 to all Army beneficiaries, it was about 900,000 at that time. Last year, 2016, we delivered 2.1 million visits to Army beneficiaries, more than double the number of people and number of times that we have been able to see people.

So I think our data shows that this issue is getting better. The core of our approach has been to move health care further forward to eliminate barriers to that care, and we have seen soldiers and their beneficiaries use it more frequently.

Mr. COFFMAN. Captain Johnson.

Captain JOHNSON. Sir, we have changed the way we do business to meet this need. Specifically, we have provided education to service members about the signs and symptoms of TBI and PTSD and, moreover, that it is a real, important issue. We have provided education to healthcare providers.

We have also changed the way we do business in theater. Historically, if a service member had a problem, they may or may not go to medical. Now, it is an event-driven process. If you are in the proximity of a blast, you are to go to medical, regardless of your symptoms, and then the healthcare provider then can get history. They have more training to determine if you did indeed sustain a TBI or have PTSD or other medical issues.

In addition, at Naval Hospital Camp Lejeune, through the Intrepid Spirit, because of our holistic, integrated, interdisciplinary approach with a standard evaluation, individualized treatment, most of the service members return to duty, so 90 percent or so.

So their testimony when they tell other service members that they went to the Intrepid Spirit and that they had these symptoms and they got better is very, very powerful. And I think, ultimately, they are our greatest advocates that say that this is a real phenomena, it is treatable, and they should seek treatment.

Mr. COFFMAN. Thank you, Captain Johnson.

Ranking Member Speier.

Ms. SPEIER. Thank you, Mr. Chairman.

As I mentioned in my earlier comments, I am concerned about the relationship between TBI and CTE [chronic traumatic encephalopathy]. There was an international state-of-the-science meeting in 2015 that agreed to six recommendations, the first of which was the creation of a coordinated brain bank and tissue repository system.

So, Captain Colston, has the DOD created or coordinated for such a repository? And, if so, how are service members informed about their opportunity to register and to donate?

Captain COLSTON. Yes, ma'am. We called Dan Perl at USUHS [Uniformed Services University of the Health Sciences] a couple days ago about this matter. He is up to 51 brains in his brain tissue repository at USUHS. Up at VA [Veterans Affairs] Boston, there are 98 brains of veterans.

So we have moved up from about a dozen to 51 at USUHS in a pretty short period, I think in about a year. The Center for Neuroregenerative Medicine [CNRM] is leading this process for DOD. And the Chronic Effects of Neurotrauma Consortium [CENC] is leading it for VA, Dave Cifu down at——

Ms. SPEIER. So how are we informing veterans and/or those who are discharged from the military of the availability of this repository?

Captain COLSTON. Right now, it is what you have on your driver's license. I know that efforts are afoot to approach that issue. Of course, what we need is brains and histories. And getting the word out is a big part of the effort at CNRM and CENC right now.

Ms. SPEIER. It sounds like we could do a better job at that than we are.

Captain COLSTON. I think the brains versus pathology progress, ma'am, is something that we need to work on. And certainly I could take that for the record.

[The information referred to can be found in the Appendix on page 69.]

Ms. SPEIER. All right.

I have been working on this issue from a different perspective for close to a decade, and I have become aware of a professor and Nobel Prize winner at UC San Francisco, Stanley Prusiner, who was the first to identify the tau protein, which is related to mad cow disease and, as a result, also related to TBIs. And he sent me this letter, which I want to read parts of it and then get your comments.

"Seemingly mild TBIs can initiate progressive nervous system degeneration involving aggregation of the tau protein into tangles within the frontal lobes of the brain. As many as one in five soldiers deployed in Iraq and Afghanistan were within the distance of an IED [improvised explosive device] blast and suffered one or more mild concussive episodes. Drugs must be developed to treat such individuals.

"Combat-related TBIs exhibit disinhibited behaviors, including depression, insomnia, drug addiction, alcoholism, and suicide. These symptoms of central nervous system dysfunction are indistinguishable from those seen in CTE patients in whom modified tau proteins aggregate. Lowering the level of tau delays the onset of neurodegeneration.

"Large numbers of service members deployed in recent conflicts will develop CTE, which is one of the subset of conditions known broadly as post-traumatic stress disorder. Hence, the identification of such drugs is an urgent medical, societal, and national security issue. The development of such medicines and that the Congress continues to fund annual research and development in the Department of Defense budget to undertake this important work is key."

So I guess my question to each of you—and I have 1 minute and 15 seconds left—is: What are we doing in terms of seeking out medicines, and to what degree do you concur with Dr. Prusiner on his conclusions?

Captain COLSTON. Ma'am, I was honored to meet Dr. Prusiner in the Assistant Secretary's office. Right now, he is working on a novel drug discovery compound, looking at about 20,000 compounds that have to do with tau aggregation. As you know, he is an expert in mad cow disease. There is a question about protein scaffolding and the progress.

The clinician in me says there probably is some nexus between TBI and CTE. But I also need to say, as a scientist, that that nexus is not fully established right now.

Ms. SPEIER. And the idea that we need a drug in order to try and address this condition in our service members?

Captain COLSTON. I think Dr. Prusiner's work is high-risk/high-reward. If, in fact, protein scaffolding is what causes CTE, I think his work will bear great fruit. As a Nobel laureate, those are the kind of people we want on high-risk/high-reward projects, and I think he is the perfect person for that job.

Ms. SPEIER. Yes, Captain Johnson.

Captain JOHNSON. At Camp Lejeune, we are making efforts to make service members more aware of the brain bank by having discussions with some of the medical leaders, both at MARSOC [Marine Corps Forces Special Operations Command] and in the MEF, the Marine Expeditionary Force, and the Special Operations Command.

In addition, I personally am donating my brain to that brain bank. And, again, I think that is one way to get the message out, that I think it is so important that I want to participate in it.

I also heard a story that I think merits discussion. There was a service member who donated his brain to the brain bank, and the family members said they felt that their son was still serving the country even after death by donating his brain to the brain repository.

So we are doing everything we can, and we support it 100 percent.

Ms. SPEIER. Colonel Pflanz.

13

Colonel PFLANZ. The Air Force is very concerned about the impact of recurrent, chronic, or severe TBI on its airmen and other service men and women. I agree with Dr. Colston that, you know, the research on the link between blast injuries and chronic traumatic encephalopathy is unclear. And, more importantly, what do we do with it once we make that link?

And so the Air Force and the other services are falling back clinically now on our DOD/VA clinical practice guidelines. Those are our bibles. You know, the latest literature, as it emerges, is incorporated into those clinical practice guidelines so that the physicians working in the trenches are using the best knowledge, best possible treatments.

Ms. SPEIER. Lieutenant Colonel Ivany.

Colonel IVANY. Ma'am, the Army recognized this as a key issue and is fully supportive of all research efforts in this area. And we feel, again, great motivation here. The Army is the lead service for the NCAA–DOD [National Collegiate Athletic Association–Department of Defense] Grand Alliance, which is a big part of the broader research assessment and following soldiers and athletes over time. And there are many other research efforts ongoing.

We feel that it is very important to continue a broad research base in this area, because the clear connections from TBI to CTE are not yet fully established. And so we feel it is important to keep many research options on the table so that we have the best chance of developing care.

Ms. SPEIER. Thank you. I yield back.

Mr. COFFMAN. I recognize Mr. Bacon for 5 minutes, and then we will have to break or recess for three votes, and then we will return to finish the hearing.

Mr. Bacon.

Mr. BACON. First of all, thank you for treating our service men and women and taking good care of them. I know, as someone who has commanded five times, the importance of what you are doing, because we have seen the impacts of when folks come back home.

I would like to ask you briefly, do you feel like you have been adequately resourced and funded to treat PTS [post-traumatic stress] and TBI?

We will start with Captain Colston.

Captain COLSTON. Yes, sir. The Defense Centers of Excellence for Psychological Health and TBI has a $125 million annual budget. I feel that is more than sufficient to meet our need. And it has helped us to do really, I think, what we need to do, which is translate theory into practice.

Mr. BACON. Thank you. Our three service reps?

Colonel PFLANZ. Sir, I would agree that we are adequately resourced to address these issues. The services are leading the way in the adoption of evidence-based therapies for PTSD. The Air Force is at 80 percent using these in treatment of PTSD, whereas many of our civilian communities are somewhere between 10 and 40 percent.

And so certainly we are being resourced—the funding that is going to Fort Detrick and our military research is tremendous. That is helping us find the cutting-edge science to advance our treatments in the field.

Mr. BACON. Great to hear.

Colonel IVANY. Sir, the Army does feel that we have good re-
sourcing in this area. We feel that the major struggle is not in having enough resources but in finding qualified mental health professionals across the country to come work with the Army at many
bases that are in places that are not necessarily highly desirable
to live.

So things in the area of a stable civilian hiring environment, lack
of CRs [continuing resolutions] and hiring freezes and those types
of things help very much with the Army to be able to use the resources that are provided to bring providers into the clinics to care
for our soldiers.

Mr. BACON. Thank you. Captain Johnson.

Captain JOHNSON. We would ask for you to continue with your
leadership, your guidance, and your commitment to helping all of
us take care of the service members and their family.

Mr. BACON. Thank you.

Here is another question. I know earlier it was harder to find effects of PTS, and I think we are trying to be a lot more aggressive
in finding it early. Do you have analysis that shows that we are
seeing a lot more earlier reporting, earlier success at finding PTS
when folks come back from deployment?

I will just start off again with Captain Colston.

Captain COLSTON. Well, sir, I think one of the first things, the
way that we approach that problem is by screening. So we do do
person-to-person mental health assessments within 90 days of the
deployment and then within 90 days after, 6 months to a year and
a half, and 1½ years to 2½ years after.

We are studying it right now. For instance, we are studying from
the standpoint of the disability evaluation system. We are studying
it from the standpoint of the prevalence of the condition. But I
don't have a final answer, because we really don't know what the
final answer is.

Mr. BACON. Uh-huh.

Colonel PFLANZ. Sir, I don't know that we can say that we are
doing a better job of identifying it earlier, but with our serial
screening, we are certainly giving airmen, soldiers, sailors, marines
an opportunity, multiple opportunities, to tell medical professionals
that they are suffering from these symptoms.

And if they are reluctant when they are first coming back from
deployment because they are worried that perhaps they might be
delayed, they have another opportunity 6 months later, and they
have another opportunity——

Mr. BACON. Right.

Colonel PFLANZ. So this serial screening is so important in giving
these airmen multiple opportunities, and that has to give us an advantage in treating these earlier.

Mr. BACON. Thank you.

Colonel IVANY. Sir, within the Army, again, this has been a
major area of focus, to try to identify these conditions as early as
possible. Screening is key. And we feel like moving care forward
has been another very important step. As I mentioned, we have
seen many more soldiers, almost twice as many, twice as fre-

quently on the outpatient side and have far fewer soldiers needing hospitalization for those same conditions.

So, for us, that is an indication that we are getting to see soldiers earlier in the course of the illness, prior to major crisis events which lead to them going into the hospital and having very negative career events.

Mr. BACON. Thank you. Captain Johnson.

Captain JOHNSON. I can just echo what my colleagues have said. There are more robust screening tools that are in use to identify service members who have TBI or PTSD earlier. The Navy has also moved forward by embedding mental health in more forward positions. So what that does is that increases access and decreases stigma.

And, finally, in our clinic, because we use a holistic, interdisciplinary, integrated approach, frequently a service member may initially say they have TBI, but then, as you get more history, PTSD due to whatever causes will become more apparent.

Mr. BACON. Well, thank you very much. I yield back my 13 seconds.

Mr. COFFMAN. Thank you, Mr. Bacon. The hearing will resume following the vote series.

[Recess.]

Mr. COFFMAN. This hearing is now called back to order.

I am still concerned about the issue of access to care and the stigma that might be—and I know you all have essentially said that access has dramatically increased, that the culture of the military has changed to where there is—you can't say no stigma, but you say—I mean, if someone is in a line position of leadership, particularly in a combat military occupational specialty, and they have got issues related to stress or TBI that they want to seek treatment on, you know, that is—that is a hard one.

And let's go back to the culture. At least I am outdated here. But, you know—but I remember, say, back when I was a junior officer, I mean, in a rifle infantry company in the Marine Corps, where if I had an appointment of any kind, the company commander was made aware of that appointment where I was leaving the company to go do something on Mainside.

So tell me about how that infantry rifle platoon commander who is expected to be—to act appropriately in a stressful environment, in a combat environment, leading marines in this particular instance, where that is not a stigma for that junior Marine officer to go to seek treatment. And it would be the same for a platoon commander of the United States Army infantry or anything in combat arms, in any—a pilot—a fighter pilot, or somebody involved in a stressful situation—in the United States Air Force or positions in the Navy. I mean, you know, if someone's a SEAL [Sea, Air, Land] team member or somebody, you know, in any kind of a combat role. I mean, what is their access to care, and is there a stigma associated to it? And do you have any ideas where legislatively we could look at changing the administrative process in terms of how somebody's healthcare record is kept and how somebody—I think you mentioned privacy issues.

So let's go back now, starting with you Captain Colston, and talk about where we are today, access today. And what can we do to improve it if, in your estimation, there needs to be something to improve access to where someone doesn't feel that there is a stigma associated with receiving care?

Captain COLSTON. Yes, sir. Well, first of all, I think you hit the nail on the head. Junior officers, and I remember my time as a junior officer, there wasn't any discussion of mental illness or suicide or anything along those lines. And also, the senior enlisted folks really do act as gatekeepers for health care. That has been one of the things that we have recognized over the years.

So the first thing is policy. So we wrote a DOD policy 6490.04 that says, it is DOD policy that mental health care is the same as a rash. Commanders need to make sure that folks view mental health care just like the sergeant coming up to you and say, hey, get that rash taken care of.

Obviously, at the unit level we need to make sure that happens. And that is where I think the embedded providers come in, the OSCAR [Operational Stress Control and Readiness] providers in the Marine Corps, the embedded behavioral health providers in the Army, the psychologists on aircraft carriers. I think that is where the role is. I think it is really—I think with regard to policy, I think we are there.

There has been talk of making all mental health care confidential. I don't know that that necessarily best balances the interests of what we need to do as a warfighting entity and meet the needs of our soldiers, sailors, airmen, and marines. But it is certainly something that we have explored and something that we have looked at in research.

One of my predecessors, Chuck Engel, has the view that that is where we should go. I think when we have kind of been through the SF–86 Question 21 with other agencies, DNI [Director of National Intelligence], those folks, I think where we are going to end up is somewhere in the middle. And I don't know what that middle is.

Mr. COFFMAN. In the civilian world, certainly in Colorado law, if a therapist has a patient who is a threat to his or herself or to someone else, then there is a reporting requirement for that.

Captain COLSTON. Yes, sir. That is commonly known as the Tarasoff warning. I am required as a psychiatrist, whether I am in the military or in the civilian world, where I have also practiced, I am required to tell folks, tell authorities if someone is a harm to themselves or others.

There has been some thought of saying, well, that is really where we should cut it off. I think when we look at it from the security standpoint, we need to be a little bit higher in DOD, though.

Mr. COFFMAN. Okay. Colonel Pflanz.

Colonel PFLANZ. Sir, American culture is changing about mental health care. The military culture is certainly changing as well. The challenge we have is that perception is ninth-tenths of reality and what airmen, soldiers, sailors, marines believe is true mobilizes their behavior. What they see is, you know, the 1 airman in 10 that goes out with a medical evaluation board, and 9 out of 10 that come back, they saw me, they had satisfactory care, they don't raise their hand and say, you know, I had a great experience with mental health.

So it is our messaging, it is our training, you know, continuing encouraging help-seeking behavior, educating airmen through suicide prevention training, resiliency training, other sorts of things that mental health care is a good thing. It doesn't have the negative outcomes, sometimes, but not usually, that they perceive it to have. And then embedding mental health closer and closer so that they are familiar with this, and the false notions that they have, they will start to learn are untrue. So again, changing perception is the most important thing. We are moving the dial, but we are not there yet.

Mr. COFFMAN. Do you think confidentiality, though, should we enhance confidentiality requirements for the patient?

Colonel PFLANZ. What I found in 22 years working with my patients is that the confidential dial is titrated to the right level. Most of my patients that I interact with that I then speak to commanders, I am an advocate for that individual. They are appreciative of that communication. And for the 95 percent of patients that I never speak to their commander, they are appreciative of that as well.

I think changing that will impair—if we make it more confidential, it will impair my opportunities to be that patient's advocate with a commander, to help that commander understand the mental illness, how it impacts the mission, and also help that commander understand that this airman with treatment is going to be a full-blown asset once we're done.

Mr. COFFMAN. Under current regulations, do you have to receive permission from the patient, the airman being treated, to be able to discuss the issue with, say, that person's commanding officer?

Colonel PFLANZ. I do not need the airman's permission for things that impact duty performance, safety, mission safety, those sorts of things.

Mr. COFFMAN. Lieutenant Colonel Ivany.

Colonel IVANY. Yes, sir. I think the key here is two things. One is a trusting, working relationship between a small number of mental health providers and then line leaders. If line leaders trust and know and understand who it is they are going to talk to themselves or who it is they are sending their soldier to talk to, they are much more likely to use that care. If we just ask them to go up to the hospital to a nameless or faceless entity and clinic and just walk in and say I need help, that is a much, much harder sell than us saying, look, please come down to the clinic two blocks down from where you work to see Dr. Johnson who has seen all your soldiers and your unit for the past, you know, couple of years and worked with you on many different issues.

So if you have a trusting working relationship, that changes the thought process, because that leader doesn't have to necessarily think differently about mental health care in general, they just have to think differently about at least one mental health provider that is there to help them and their unit. So I think that is one of the keys.

The second is that while we want to make sure that we offer as much confidentiality as possible, we have to balance readiness. So when we identify a readiness impairing issue, it is in the best interest of the unit, of the leader, and ultimately the soldier themselves to make sure that is known to the appropriate people so that we can form a community to help that soldier to get better or to help them take the next steps in their life.

Mr. COFFMAN. Captain Johnson.

Captain JOHNSON. We have found that education of the service members, as well as healthcare providers, is one way to decrease stigma. In addition, when service members are referred to the Intrepid Spirit Concussion Recovery Clinic and when they recover and when they return to full duty, that is a testimony to the fact that TBI and PTSD are real issues and they are also treatable. And it encourages service members. It gives them hope to step forward, to seek treatment, and then return and get back into the fight.

Mr. COFFMAN. Thank you very much.

Ms. McSally, you are now recognized for 5 minutes.

Ms. MCSALLY. Thank you, Mr. Chairman. And thank you, gentlemen, for your service and your care for our troops.

I am a big proponent of integrated medicine and—for myself and really from a public policy point of view. And alternative options are just sometimes challenging because they are not recognized often in the medical community. So can you speak a little bit more about—you know, I have talked to organizations that are involved with helping our troops, this is mostly with vets, hyperbaric oxygen therapy, or another organization our community is involved in, take and choose for PTSD on, you know, doing scuba-related underwater therapy, or service animals, other nontraditional things that there is, again, outside organizations that are already doing things like this. Sometimes it is tougher for a big bureaucracy to accept some of these alternative things that they say can't be proven.

So just talk to me about some of the things that you might be working on or you think that may be useful. I have seen it in some of your testimony, Captain Johnson. Any other perspectives on these other treatments. Some of them, again, may be psychological, but also there is some physiological elements, I think, of a cortisol. And I am not a doctor, but other things related to the potential benefits for those that are suffering from PTSD and TBI.

Captain JOHNSON. You have hit on a very important issue. Just to break down your question to the components, in regards to hyperbaric oxygen therapy, currently, the FDA [Food and Drug Administration] has I believe it is 13 approved indications for the use of hyperbaric oxygen therapy. The Navy and the DOD provides clinical care for these approved uses of hyperbaric oxygen therapy. So our use of hyperbaric oxygen therapy is in alignment with the FDA and the Undersea and Hyperbaric Medical Society. Having said that, there is always more to learn, and we certainly are open to discussion to explore research and other projects that involve hyperbaric oxygen that can help service members and their families.

In regards to complementary and integrated medicine, we have found at Camp Lejeune that service members are very receptive to it. They are hesitant about taking a pill. We use a lot of acupuncture, yoga, various meditation techniques, Alpha stimulation, audio-visual entrainment, and various other tools. We have found that this results in a decreased need for medications, in particular, narcotics. It is a central part of our treatment plan.

Ms. McSALLY. Are you bringing in experts from off base in order to partner with that or are you building expertise within the service?

Captain JOHNSON. Both.

Ms. McSALLY. Okay.

Captain JOHNSON. For example, myself and one of my colleagues in the clinic has completed training in acupuncture. But we also have relationships through our NICoE [National Intrepid Center of Excellence] and Intrepid Spirit's network to discuss the latest and newest innovations in complementary and innovative medicine.

Ms. McSALLY. Great. Thanks. Captain Colston, did you have something to add?

Captain COLSTON. Yes, ma'am. We welcome complementary and alternative medicine in DOD. And, in fact, given the national opiate scourge, I think especially for pain disorders it is important to have yoga and acupuncture and mindfulness and other therapies available for patients. And I think—if I were to look at family practice docs across the board right now, lots of them are trained in battlefield acupuncture where we really are using it.

Ms. McSALLY. Yeah. Is there also, as you are—maybe again this breaks up our thinking on some traditional mindsets, right, transitioning that to the VA, are you—I mean, are we seeing partnering with the VA to make sure, if you guys are all using this and it is working, as they are transitioning, they are not dealing with similar bureaucracy saying, sorry, that is not approved, we don't do that here? Anybody else want to jump in?

Colonel PFLANZ. I think that, you know, all the services are interested in the emerging research, and our partnership with the VA and our clinical practice guidelines is one of our great strengths. It makes us, despite our size, a very nimble organization as new research emerges. And almost all of our research projects are partnered with civilian institutions, so we have the best minds out there assisting us. And as this new research emerges, it is incorporated relatively quickly into our clinical practice guidelines. The one on PTSD is being updated as we speak, and that allows our practitioners in the field to have the cutting-edge tools to treat airmen, soldiers, sailors, marines in those clinics with the best possible science that has emerged.

Ms. McSALLY. You have got to believe there is skepticism within the traditional medical community, right, on some of these things? I deal with it all the time. Right? So how are you overcoming that?

Lieutenant Colonel Ivany, is that how you say it? Do you want to jump in?

Colonel IVANY. Yes, ma'am. I think that the more that we put these alternative approaches out in clearly defined clinical practice guidelines, which is the clear state of the science that is a joint DOD/VA work, then more and more people out there in each individual clinic will see that this is clearly beneficial and this is not a competition. It is an augmentation to what they are doing to help their patients.

Ms. McSALLY. Great. Thank you. I am over my time. I appreciate all of your work, gentlemen. Thank you. I yield back.

Mr. COFFMAN. Thank you, Ms. McSally.

Ranking Member Speier.

Ms. SPEIER. Thank you. I just have a couple of quick questions.

Lieutenant Colonel Ivany, you referenced in your statement that one of your biggest problems was hiring, that you have a 15 percent turnover rate with your specialists who provide the services. And I can see for the service member having to redevelop a relationship with yet another behavioral specialist has got to be problematic. What can we do to fix that?

Colonel IVANY. Ma'am, I think the biggest thing that we can do is to make sure that the healthcare providers who have options to work with us or work elsewhere have trust that there is a stable hiring environment within the U.S. Government and within the Army. So that—for instance, the recent hiring freeze, you know, as we identify and try to bring providers on, we had to have many of those providers wait. And they weren't able to come onboard to our clinics until we have worked through the steps to resolve the hiring freeze to get them through the gate.

So they are hesitant to hear about sequestration. They hear about continuing resolutions, and it makes many hesitant. So I think that is the single most important thing at the national level that would help us at the clinical level.

Ms. SPEIER. All right. Captain Johnson, you talked about some of those suffering from TBIs or PTSD self-medicating. I am presuming this is alcohol and drugs, unrelated to their condition. Is that right?

Captain JOHNSON. That is correct.

Ms. SPEIER. I have a lot of biotech in my district. And I was speaking to one of my CEOs just last night who said that they are close to finding a genetic marker for PTSD. Are you looking at that at all in the research that is being undertaken? And if not, why not?

Captain COLSTON. Yes, ma'am. In fact, we have protocols underway right now to look at genetic loci for PTSD. I just say there are far more than one, and that is one of the things that we find across mental illness, across PTSD, depression, autism spectrum disorders. But we have funded research and we are looking at that closely.

Ms. SPEIER. My colleague had to leave, but Congresswoman Shea-Porter is from New Hampshire where the opioid crisis has been particularly severe. And she got the impression from your testimony, and maybe it was you, Captain Colston, who talked about the success you are having. And she wants to know if there are certain procedures or policies or programs you have undertaken that has been particularly successful, could you share them with us? And if you could do that for the record, that would be helpful.

Captain COLSTON. Yes, ma'am. Well, I would start with it is my opinion, but I think the fact that our death rate is 2.7 per 100,000, and the national death rate is 10.4 for 100,000, for opiates, is obviously a significant difference between populations. Universally, we have random drug testing, which is, of course, not available to most people. You know, in regard to civil rights that you have when you are an Active Duty service member, there is a difference between being a civilian and in the military.

I do think secondary prevention efforts are really where we have excelled with regard to pharmacy interventions, a prescription drug tracking system, various issues with regards to sole provider pro- grams. And then goalkeepers, to be quite honest with you, ma'am.

One of the things that I do as a psychiatrist, that I have a bupre- norphine waiver. So I can give medication-assisted therapy for peo- ple who are addicted to opiates, give them a drug that they can't overdose on, give them a drug that they can't snort and, hence, die. I think that has been useful. And, of course, we have put naloxone into the hands of first responders. And in New England, New Hampshire, Vermont, Governor—I know the Governor in Vermont made the entire state of his governorship address one year on opi- ate overdose deaths.

This is the single biggest public health crisis that we have faced. It is 55,000 overdose deaths a year. Car accidents, 38,000; gun deaths, 36,000. AIDS was never this big. It is a huge issue. And frankly, it is a doctor-created problem and it is on us to fix it.

Ms. SPEIER. Last question I have. To what extent are we now tracking those who have been diagnosed with TBI over the course of the rest of their lives to see what conditions they acquire that we would attribute to TBI?

Captain COLSTON. So we have two studies underway. We have the 15-year longitudinal TBI study, which we are 7 years into. And I think that is going to talk an awful lot especially about how PTSD and TBI and suicidality and chronic pain and substance use all overlap. And we will learn a lot more about that. We also have an IMAP [Improved Understanding of Medical and Psychological Needs in Veterans and Service Members with TBI] study. In re- gard to the here and now, how do we look at—how do we look at TBI. Well, we have a very robust surveillance network with regard to TBI, and we look at scientifically something called incidence, which is new incidents and prevalence. In other words, how people are—if people aren't recovering from TBI.

Most TBI is self limiting. Most mild TBI just gets better. It doesn't matter if you saw a doctor, it doesn't matter what you do. What we need to get on top of are the chronic cases, and we need to learn about those.

Ms. SPEIER. So do you think the studies are going to provide you with that?

Captain COLSTON. Yes, ma'am. I think longitudinal studies are really the way to go. The Framingham study, really, we learned a ton about coronary artery disease. I think the Army's STARRS [Study to Assess Risk and Resilience in Servicemembers] study in regard to suicide is going to yield great benefit. I think longitudinal studies like the Millennium Cohort Study, which in essence is a study that looks at what does military service do to you health- wise—I think they are all extremely important.

Ms. SPEIER. Okay. Thank you. Thank you, Mr. Chairman.

Mr. COFFMAN. Thank you, Ms. Speier.

I wish to thank the witnesses for their testimony this afternoon. This has been very informative.

There being no further businesses, the subcommittee stands ad- journed.

[Whereupon, at 4:12 p.m., the subcommittee was adjourned.]

APPENDIX

APRIL 27, 2017

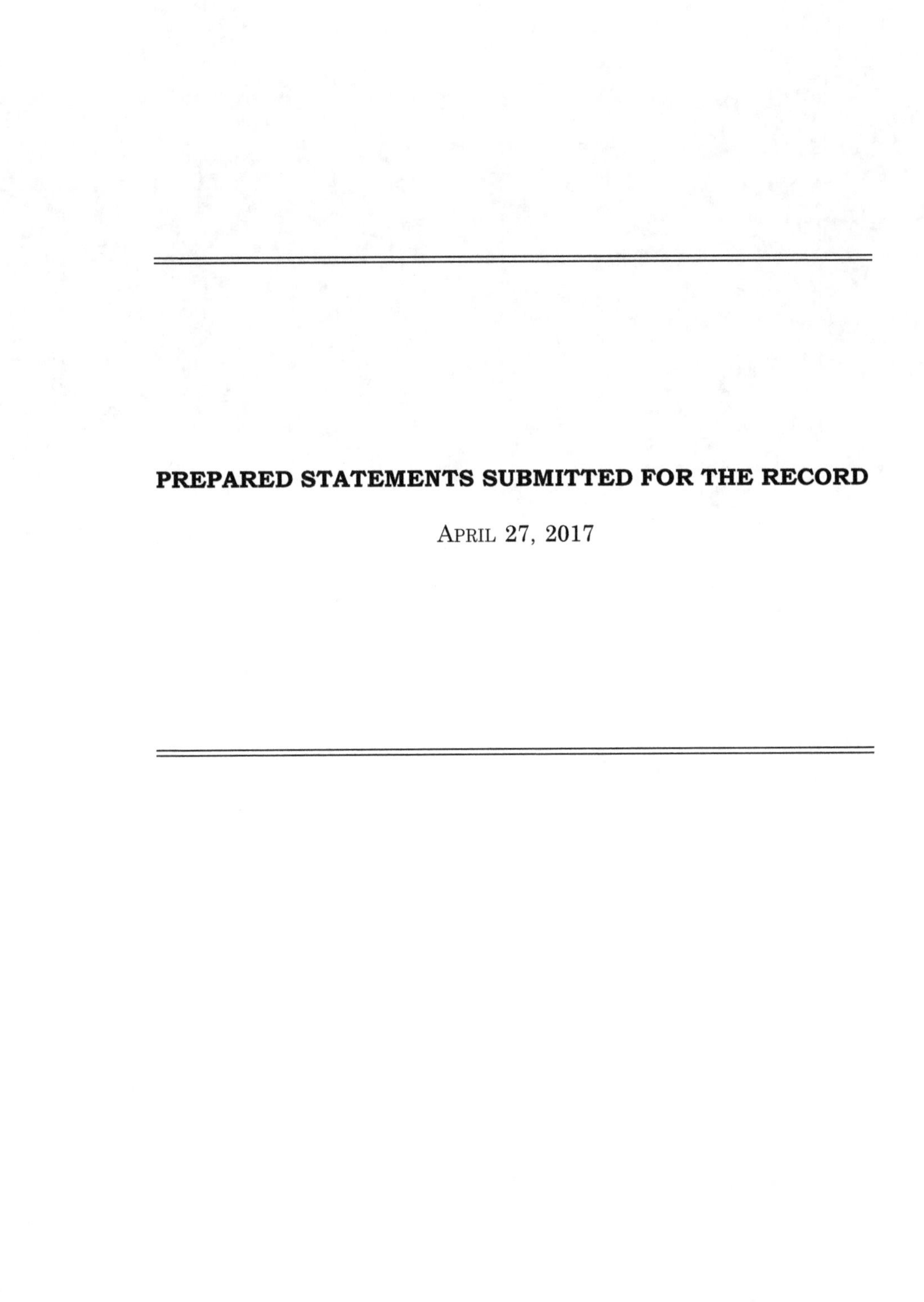

PREPARED STATEMENTS SUBMITTED FOR THE RECORD

APRIL 27, 2017

Opening Remarks – Chairman Coffman
Military Personnel Subcommittee Hearing

PTSD and TBI—Clinical and Research Program Assessment

April 27, 2017

The hearing will come to order.

Good afternoon and welcome. Today the subcommittee will hear from the Department of Defense and the military departments on their efforts to address the effects of post-traumatic stress disorder (PTSD) and traumatic brain injury (TBI) on our service members. For far too long, the real and proven effects of PTSD and TBI largely were ignored. Even worse, service members who demonstrated symptoms of PTSD were sometimes deemed weak or mentally unstable. Thankfully, we know better today and are taking aggressive steps to help those who have endured traumatic stress.

As a nation, we've endured an extraordinarily long period of conflict, with thousands of American troops deployed in harm's way. Some, as a result of their combat experiences, suffer from post-traumatic stress or TBI. But PTSD and TBI are not limited to combat injuries. PTSD can arise from any traumatic event, such as sexual assault. We expect the Department to treat all those suffering from PTSD or TBI equally, providing the best appropriate care for each.

For more than a decade, Congress has provided funding and legislative direction for the Department's PTSD and TBI research and clinical approaches. In fact, relevant provisions of law are found in each of the last four NDAAs. Today, our intent is to review our progress and determine where we need to go from here. Our witnesses are experts in the field of mental health, and I look forward to hearing their views of our clinical and research progress. If they have any suggestions for the subcommittee, I welcome them.

Before I introduce the witnesses, I'd like to turn to Ranking Member Speier for any opening comments she would like to make.

(27)

Prepared Statement

of

Captain Mike Colston, M.D.

**Director, Defense Centers of Excellence for
Psychological Health and Traumatic Brain Injury**

REGARDING

**THE CURRENT STATE AND FUTURE AIMS OF PSYCHOLOGICAL HEALTH AND
TRAUMATIC BRAIN INJURY—CLINICAL AND RESEARCH PROGRAM
ASSESSMENT**

BEFORE THE

**HOUSE ARMED SERVICES COMMITTEE
SUBCOMMITTEE ON MILITARY PERSONNEL**

APRIL 27, 2017

Not for publication until released by the Committee

Chairman Coffman, Ranking Member Speier, and members of the Committee, thank you for the opportunity to discuss the Department of Defense's (DoD's) efforts to promote psychological health and to prevent, diagnose, and treat Traumatic Brain Injury (TBI), posttraumatic stress disorder (PTSD) and associated mental health conditions . I am honored to join my colleagues from the Army, Navy and Air Force for today's testimony.

I would like to thank the Committee for its sustained leadership and support for the work we perform in the Military Health System (MHS) to care for our Nation's Service members, veterans, and their families—especially those dealing with complex issues related to mental health and TBI. Your investments in medical research have led to important advances in care and a greater understanding of where future research should be targeted.

The MHS' overriding mission—centered on readiness—is to ensure a medically ready force and a ready medical force. This mission has grown in complexity. As our advances shed new light on our principal areas of research, we also are confronting new medical challenges every day—from developing more sophisticated capabilities that increase survivability from trauma, to treating Ebola and other infectious diseases, to creating advanced prosthetics that aid in the recovery of our wounded and injured Service members. All the while, we are addressing threats in the arenas of PTSD and other mental health issues, TBI, suicide and substance use.

Although the MHS is still learning and striving to treat mental health illness more effectively, we are one of the only health systems in the Nation that is reliably obtaining outcomes for the treatment of mental health conditions, and we are a leader in treating severe mental illness in the population of young adults who often present with these illnesses for the first time. RAND validated much of DoD's progress in a recently published a report on the quality of care for Posttraumatic Stress Disorder (PTSD) and depression in the MHS. The MHS continues to outperform civilian health care systems by ensuring that patients with PTSD or depression receive an outpatient follow-up visit within 7 to 30 days after psychiatric hospitalization. Over 87% of patients received a follow-up visit within 7 days, and over 95% received this visit within 30 days. Additionally, in new treatment episodes, the MHS demonstrated high rates of assessment for suicide risk—96%in a PTSD cohort and 88% in a depression cohort—and high rates of assessment for substance use—93% in a PTSD cohort and 90 % in a depression cohort.

DoD has sustained efforts to track the long-term effects of TBI. In 2009, the Secretary of Defense directed the Defense and Veterans Brain Injury Center, a component of DCoE, to address DoD's portion of the "Longitudinal Study on Traumatic Brain Injury Incurred by Members of the Armed Forces in Operation IRAQI FREEDOM and Operation ENDURING FREEDOM." DCoE is responsible for two component studies within this directive. The first, "The 15-Year Studies," focuses on the long-term physical and mental health needs of Service members, veterans, and their families. The second, "Improved Understanding of Medical and Psychological Needs in Service Members and Veterans with Chronic Traumatic Brain Injury," or "IMAP," examines the rehabilitation and health care needs of Service members and veterans with TBI.

Both the "15-Year Studies" and the "IMAP" make it clear that comorbidities—such as PTSD, acute stress, and sleep disruption—complicate TBI recovery and create a need for a complementary suite of mental health and rehabilitation services for effective TBI treatment. The studies also identify variation in effective treatments for male versus female Service members and highlight the necessity of providing services and training to family members.

The year 2017 marks the seven-year update on the 15 year study. Our work reflects the collaborative efforts of DoD, other government agencies, academic research institutions, and the private sector.

DoD is engaged in an ongoing fight to improve mental health and stem suicide deaths among our Service members. We have established programs and policies intended to prevent suicide, as well as a behavioral health database, the Behavioral Health Data Portal (BHDP), which tracks the effectiveness of clinical interventions in the MHS. In addition, my office, the Defense Centers of Excellence for Psychological Health and Traumatic Brain Injury (DCoE), has nearly finished its structured five-year evaluation of many non-clinical mental health efforts, including suicide prevention programs. We will share preliminary findings today. Based on these findings, we are helping focus clinical research on both predicting suicide and responding to suicidal behavior.

Throughout the United States, a new and complex health issue has appeared in our communities—an epidemic of opioid overdose deaths. DoD has instituted scientifically informed, effective policies and clinical guidance to reduce opioid abuse and overdose deaths within its ranks. In 2016, 2,148 Active Duty Service members had a diagnosis of Opioid Use Disorder, a decrease of 38% from 2012. Likewise, opiate positive drug tests among Active Duty Service members declined over 60% between fiscal year (FY) 2013 and FY 2016. Finally, in 2015, there were 35 deaths among Active Duty Service members from opioid overdose (2.7 deaths per 100,000 Active Duty Service members): while even one overdose is one too many, this was approximately one-fourth of the general U.S. population rate, and even less of a fraction of the rate in an age- and sex-matched cohort.

Current State of Evaluating Treatment for Mental Health Conditions and TBI

In FY 2013, directorates in the Office of the Assistant Secretary of Defense for Health Affairs compiled a list of 377 possible programs, both line and medical, with a nexus to psychological health, substance use disorders, suicide and TBI to review for inclusion in a program evaluation process. In an iterative process through FY2014, several programs—about 160, were removed from the list because they no longer received DoD funding, they were no longer in existence, or they were folded into other programs. Of the remaining 210 programs, approximately 35 more were removed between FY 14 and FY 17 because they did not meet or no longer met inclusion criteria for the review. The current total is approximately 175. OSD CAPE has requested the individual Services review final findings when available and make determinations regarding any program modifications including redundancies or discontinuation.

The effectiveness of the remaining DoD-funded psychological health, TBI, substance use and suicide prevention programs, is addressed below. About 30 mental health programs use "train-the-trainer" methods that encourage the use of best practices to deliver assistance to Service members at risk of suicide or behavioral health problems. Our evaluation confirmed the importance of fostering a community of acceptance and de-stigmatizing the act of seeking assistance for mental health issues. The effectiveness of these programs depends greatly on the instructors' capabilities, as well as adaptability in meeting the needs of target populations. To date, there is a dearth of good data supporting the effectiveness of many peer-to-peer interventions. The program evaluation initiative identifies efforts that are not achieving success and helps to focus our work on the most promising interventions.

DoD is likewise learning important lessons about suicide response programs, which often provide short-term support to individuals exposed to traumatic events. These programs foster resilience and unit cohesion by providing education, stabilization, and referrals to resources; according to our initial findings from program evaluations, they enjoy support from the communities served. Yet outcomes are challenging to systematically track. Although many programs track output metrics (e.g., participant counts, demographics) and obtain feedback from participants through mechanisms such as participant surveys, the need to both standardize metrics and also improve monitoring that better assesses successful initiatives is urgent.

Of course, the outcome measure that matters most in suicide is the death rate, which remains unacceptably high despite years of sustained effort at prevention and intervention. The DoD Suicide Event Report surveillance system collects data on every suicide that occurs while a Service member is in a duty status within the Active, Reserve, and National Guard Components of the Air Force, Army, Navy, and Marine Corps. This system has been in operation since calendar year (CY) 2008. This system reports that there has been no measureable change, neither increase nor decrease, in the annual suicide rate for Active Duty Service members since 2009. Data from CY 2015 and preliminary data from CY 2016 suggest that roughly 1 in 5,000 Active Duty Service members died by suicide in the last two years. The rate was approximately 1 in 4,000 between the combined National Guard and Reserve forces. Similarly, raw counts of the occurrence of suicide from 2016 show that Active Duty deaths had increased by 10 cases from 2015 but had not changed in a statistically significant manner from the 4 years prior.

Trends in suicide remain disturbing, as does the loss of the "warrior effect." This "warrior effect" once seemed to protect a DoD cohort because such a cohort was employed, screened at accession for common mental illnesses, and primed for ongoing leadership intervention as well as the most extensive array of psychosocial support in the history of public health.

Future of Mental Health and TBI Research, Treatment, and Therapies

We are encouraged by the successes DoD has seen in combatting the opioid crisis and by improvements in assessment and treatment of PTSD and TBI that stem from attention to outcome data. Likewise, DoD strives to improve its program evaluation and knowledge translation systems. These systems work in tandem to ensure that the best evidence-based practices make their way from researchers to the field as efficiently as possible.

DoD implemented its Behavioral Health Data Portal (BHDP) across many clinical mental health programs to better standardize data collection and reporting measures. A computerized patient kiosk collects baseline and follow-up data on symptoms related to common mental health conditions (e.g., depression, anxiety). It augments the MHS' existing electronic health record system by efficiently tracking, sorting, and filtering information about mental health treatment and outcomes. The BHDP allows for real-time graphing of outcome measures for clinical care, consolidation of data from multiple sources into one clinician dashboard, and aggregation of data for meaningful program evaluation. Collated data across multiple programs is allowing DoD to determine the effectiveness of mental health programs in real time.

Medical research, on the other hand, takes time: advances accrue in an unpredictable course, and findings are published at a volume and rate that often outpaces clinicians' ability to adopt best practices. Studies show that it often takes 15 years or more to incorporate a medical discovery into clinical care and policy. Fortunately, the MHS is uniquely positioned to address this public health challenge as an integrated health delivery system: we directly fund the research, assess the findings, educate and train our medical workforce, and operate a global health care delivery system for our patients. As a result, we have the potential to create a comprehensive model that moves evidence-based findings from bench to bedside rapidly.

To this end, DCoE developed a generalizable, evidence-based knowledge translation process for use in the MHS. This capability provides a standardized process for the targeted synthesis, analysis, translation, dissemination, and implementation of psychological health and TBI research into evidence-based practices and consistent standards of care. Having a functional and standardized knowledge translation process for mental health care may also herald advancements in MHS practices beyond psychological health and TBI.

Line and Medical Interventions to Combat Opioid Addiction

DoD is succeeding in combatting opiate addiction through sustained leadership efforts that focus on readiness and relentless attention to innovations in medical practice.

As mentioned, positive drug screens are down 60%, despite upgraded screening capabilities to detect metabolites of commonly abused prescription opiates. DoD's dedication to a drug free workplace, its culture of involved leadership and care for its Service members, and its vigilance in its detection of and care for Service members who struggle with substance abuse have led to trends that starkly contrast the worsening national scourge in recent years.

In cooperation with our interagency partners, DoD is working with prescribers and providers to address pain-management practices that contribute to abuse and addiction. We are expanding access to effective treatment options. We are putting tools into the hands of first responders—including opioid overdose reversal with naloxone—that are helping save the lives of overdose victims. We are simultaneously intensifying our outreach and education efforts.

Let me highlight some specifics. Appropriate pain management plays a critical role in preventing opioid abuse. In November 2016, DoD implemented its Opioid Prescriber Safety Training Program to improve patient outcomes in pain management and substance abuse. As of mid-April, more than 14,000 DoD prescribers completed this training, and all remaining prescribers are on track to complete training by September 2017. Rapid progress stemmed from medical leadership's focused attention and the ease of use of our online training programs, which automatically generate medical education credits for users. Plainly, urgency and technological innovation allowed DoD to scale-up training rapidly to meet the crisis. We hope to replicate this approach as we create new trainings for other clinical programs.

In 2013, we began two Joint Incentive Fund Projects to expand access to and use of non-opioid treatments for acute and chronic pain. The first, a $2.5M initiative we developed with VA, is a joint pain management curriculum to improve the pain management competencies of the federal clinical workforce. Its goal is to help reduce opioid overuse—and it is scheduled to be completed in August 2017. The second, a $3.1M initiative, developed, evaluated, and implemented a uniform tiered acupuncture education and training program (ATACS). The ATACS project was completed in August 2016. Evidence-based, non-pharmacological treatments such as acupuncture, movement therapy, or massage can effectively treat pain, and we want to ensure that providers are aware of—and prescribe—these services for patients. Finally, we established an MHS Opioid Registry to provide decision-makers with real-time data that track and monitor patients at risk for misuse, abuse, and overdose.

DoD is taking significant steps to improve the access and the options available to patients living with the horrors of addiction. Last September, DoD issued TRICARE regulations that greatly expand coverage for medication-assisted treatment of opioid use disorder. This change made coverage available for therapies certified by our partners at the Substance Abuse and Mental Health Services Administration, such as buprenorphine and methadone. We increased the number of Drug Enforcement Administration-certified buprenorphine prescribers at our Military Treatment Facilities. Over the last 2 years, 182 prescribers received training. Another 120 will receive training this year. DoD will continue to expand access to this treatment, in compliance with legislation enacted last year permitting physician assistants and nurse practitioners to prescribe buprenorphine.

DoD continues to enhance our prevention, education, and outreach programs for Service members and their families. These efforts include classroom training, public service announcements, and online and social media campaigns. DoD codified one such outreach effort last year: the Drug Take Back Program, which seeks to remove medication from circulation that could potentially be used in suicide attempts, misuse, diversion, or accidental poisoning.

Though we have taken great measures to implement improvements across the spectrum from research to care, a continued and sustained effort is necessary to fight this epidemic. Continued collaboration at the interagency level will ensure that best practices and research make their way to clinicians and practitioners in the field.

Conclusion

With Congress' steadfast support for our research and operational requirements, we are making progress—but we are not claiming victory. The challenges faced by those we serve are life-long, and they demand our unwavering commitment to best practices grounded in public health principles, scientific research and discovery. We look forward to keeping Committee apprised of our progress, and I look forward to answering your questions.

Navy Capt. (Dr.) Mike Colston
Director, Defense Centers of Excellence for Psychological Health and
Traumatic Brain Injury

Navy Capt. (Dr.) Mike Colston is the DCoE director. He is responsible for the work of approximately 600 employees at DCoE headquarters and centers who work to improve the lives of our nation's service members, families and veterans by advancing excellence in the prevention and care of psychological health conditions and traumatic brain injury.

Colston joined the Navy as a line officer, serving as a nuclear engineer and surface warfare officer aboard USS Carl Vinson (CVN-70), deploying twice to the Arabian Sea and completing a Pacific Rim Exercise. Transitioning to the Medical Corps, he earned a medical degree from the Uniformed Services University of the Health Sciences; trained as a resident in psychiatry at Walter Reed Army Medical Center, Bethesda, Maryland; and completed a fellowship in child and adolescent psychiatry at Northwestern University in Chicago. Colston holds a Bachelor of Science degree in Industrial and Management Engineering from Rensselaer Polytechnic Institute and a master's degree in Marine Affairs from the University of Rhode Island.

In previous medical corps assignments, Colston served as Chief of the Mental Health Department at Naval Hospital Great Lakes, overseeing a large-scale clinical integration that led to merged VA-DoD services at the Lovell Federal Health Care Center. During deployment in support of Operation Enduring Freedom, he led a combat and operational stress team that supported a catchment of 10,000 service members. As director of the Mental Health Program in the Office of the Assistant Secretary of Defense for Health Affairs, Colston managed a mental health board project that reviewed over 200,000 cases involving posttraumatic stress disorder (PTSD) and depression diagnoses, led a mental health team in the independent investigation of the 2013 Washington Navy Yard tragedy, and co-chaired the Defense Department Addictive Substances Misuse Advisory Committee, helping address a nationwide scourge of opiate addiction on several fronts.

Colston is an experienced leader and speaker representing the Defense Department in testimony to Congress and presidential executive offices including the Office of National Drug Control Policy, the Domestic Policy Council, and the National Security Council. Colston served on research advisory boards for the Congressionally-directed Medical Research Program, the Military Suicide Research Consortium and the National Institutes of Health National Advisory Council on Neurological Disorders and Stroke. As an author, Colston wrote a chapter on the forensic aspects of PTSD in the "Textbook of Military Medicine" series, and is published in peer-reviewed journals on topics including uncertainties in diagnosis and treatment of mental illnesses and bioethical considerations related to research in psychological health; traumatic brain injury; and suicide.

Colston is credentialed at Fort Belvoir Community Hospital, Virginia, is board certified in child and adolescent psychiatry, and has practiced in inpatient, outpatient and step- down addiction settings. His military awards and decorations include the Defense Superior Service Medal, the Office of the Secretary of Defense Badge, Surface Warfare and Officer-in-Charge Afloat devices, and campaign medals and ribbons spanning four overseas operations.

40

DEPARTMENT OF THE AIR FORCE

PRESENTATION TO THE SUBCOMMITTEE ON MILITARY PERSONNEL

COMMITTEE ON ARMED SERVICES

UNITED STATES HOUSE OF REPRESENTATIVES

SUBJECT: POST-TRAUMATIC STRESS DISORDER/TRAUMATIC BRAIN INJURY

STATEMENT OF:

COLONEL STEVEN E. PFLANZ
DIRECTOR OF PSYCHOLOGICAL HEALTH,
UNITED STATES AIR FORCE MEDICAL SUPPORT AGENCY

APRIL 27, 2017

Chairman Coffman, Ranking Member Speier, and distinguished members of the Subcommittee, thank you for inviting me to testify before you today.

The most valuable Air Force assets are the men and women who operate and maintain the systems that enable our air, space, and cyberspace missions. As such, we have a duty to support, protect, and nurture those we work beside to ensure every Airman is capable of maximum performance in support of our national security objectives, and that no Airman suffers unnecessarily under the burden of disease.

Over the last decade, we have come to understand Post-Traumatic Stress Disorder (PTSD) and Traumatic Brain Injury (TBI) as Invisible Wounds. While these wounds are not always visible to other people, they are not invisible for those who are suffering from them. These conditions impose significant challenges for the Airmen who have received these diagnoses. Accordingly, we remain focused on ensuring our Total Force Airmen receive world-class care from the point of injury or illness through their return to duty, separation, or retirement.

Despite our sustained high operational tempo, the rate of PTSD in Airmen has remained relatively low: the calendar year 2016 PTSD incidence rate was 6.8 per 1,000 active duty members, and the five-year average PTSD rate among active duty Airmen is 6.2 per 1,000 members, slightly higher than the 10-year average of 5.2 per 1,000 members. Aeromedical operational studies conducted by the US Air Force School of Aerospace Medicine from 2011 to 2017 reveal that 2 - 14% of Airmen meet mental health diagnostic criteria for PTSD. These studies found that the higher the exposure to battlefield trauma and violence, the greater the elevated risk. Of all active duty members who experienced combat exposure during deployment in 2016, a total of 25% received a diagnosis of PTSD.

While our overall rate of PTSD has remained low, we have seen gradually increasing numbers of Airmen with new diagnoses. This is not surprising given the sustained conflicts facing our nation and the increased awareness of mental health issues in our force, particularly regarding the importance of receiving treatment. As our ability to identify Invisible Wounds increases and mental health stigma decreases, we anticipate a continued increase in the rate of diagnosis of and treatment for these disorders.

Regardless of the origin of the injury, the Air Force remains committed to helping Airmen with PTSD and TBI through enhanced prevention messaging, improvements in early symptom recognition, and development of highly effective treatments. Our focus is on developing the most effective processes to help Airmen recover and return to full function, both personally and professionally.

Over the last 15 years, deployed mental health providers have been making advances in the field-based adaptation of evidence-based treatments for PTSD. These enhancements include combining therapeutic components in novel ways to meet operational demands and unique client attributes. This pioneering work has led to several testable models of PTSD treatment. One example is an evidence-based four-session protocol for treating PTSD in primary care clinics, which allows providers to deliver care to patients through a coordinated medical team. Another example is cognitive behavior therapy. This therapy focuses explicitly on traumatic memory processing, a form of treatment that has robust research support across numerous studies. In the area of treating Acute Stress Disorder, we continue to screen our Airmen for PTSD symptoms at various points in the deployment cycle and have improved resilience training for our Airmen prior to deployment. We are also working to implement additional in-theater screening for traumatic stress conditions to identify service members who may benefit from early intervention before they develop into PTSD.

Airmen in career fields at higher risk for developing PTSD receive targeted education and training on how to recognize PTSD symptoms and access available resources. In order to expand awareness, the Air Force is developing an educational initiative that will encourage early help-seeking and teach Airmen the skills necessary to more effectively identify and respond to members with PTSD and TBI.

In addition to the advances in care delivery that have been made over the last decade, the Air Force is committed to advancing the state of science to optimize treatment for members with Invisible Wounds. To that end, we are conducting several PTSD research trials with funding from the Defense Health Program's Psychological Health & Traumatic Brain Injury Research Program. This research is conducted in collaboration with the University of Texas Health Science Center in San Antonio, Texas, and involves world-wide recruitment of Air Force members with co-investigators at several Air Force installations. One focus area is a brief therapy approach based on the use of written summaries of a patient's trauma. Another study will compare different lengths of treatment sessions associated with evidence-based psychotherapies. For example, one form of evidence-based treatment, Prolonged Exposure Therapy, employs repeated exposure to thoughts, memories, and other stimuli associated with a traumatic event. This treatment is typically delivered in 90-minute therapy sessions. However, researchers are exploring whether the same treatment can be delivered in 60-minute sessions with equal efficacy.

Another active research project underway is exploring the usefulness of in-home Cognitive Processing Therapy, which has been found to decrease PTSD symptoms through helping patients correct maladaptive thoughts that have developed as a result of traumatic exposure. Delivering this treatment in a self-directed home-based model may empower the patient while decreasing barriers to care that result from perceived mental health stigma. Research participants in all these studies include service members and veterans with combat-related PTSD.

The Air Force is also engaged in a Department of Defense double-blind study, funded by the Army Medical Research Acquisition Activity, on the use of stellate ganglion blocks for PTSD treatment. This form of treatment blocks nerve fibers at the base of the neck to decrease the "fight or flight" response and has the potential to reduce symptoms of PTSD related to emotional hyper-arousal.

For those Airmen in uniquely stressed career fields, the Air Force has successfully embedded Mental Health and Primary Care providers into select units such as explosive ordnance disposal, remotely piloted aircraft (RPA) and intelligence units. Over the last six years, operational support teams comprised of medical and/or behavioral health experts have been embedded in select locations to provide continuous, direct support with successful outcomes. Based on unit surveys completed during this period, there has been a decrease in suicidal ideation from 2% to 1%, a decline in medically significant psychological distress from 25% to 15%, and partner-relational problems are down from 75% to 23%.

In addition, under the Behavioral Health Optimization Program, known as BHOP, mental health clinicians have been integrated into all Air Force primary care clinics. This facilitates the delivery of mental health care in a less stigmatizing environment for service members and their families, helping to provide "the right care at the right time in the right place." Research on our BHOP has demonstrated marked improvement in reported symptoms, cost effectiveness, and primary care provider and patient satisfaction. The program's demonstrated success has supported the rollout of this service to every Air Force medical treatment center and helped disseminate the practice, to justify bringing similar services throughout the DoD.

Air Force TBI rates also remain relatively low. The 5-year average TBI incidence rate among active duty Airmen is 0.5 per 1,000 active duty Airmen, slightly higher than the 10-year average TBI rate of 0.4 per 1,000 members. Of our TBI cases, the vast majority result from concussions, or mild TBIs, and are not combat related. Regardless of the cause, we are expanding our efforts to ensure our Airmen receive medical care for TBI. Accordingly, we identify deployed individuals with TBI symptoms upon their return from theater through the Post Deployment Health Assessment and Reassessment, with referral for additional care if and as indicated.

The Defense Centers of Excellence for Psychological Health and Traumatic Brain Injury, and the Defense and Veterans Brain Injury Center continue to serve as valuable partners in facilitating a combined effort between the Services, to develop clinical practice guidelines for providers. Additionally, the United States Air Force Academy is a participating site in the NCAA-DoD Grand Alliance, a large consortium of university and Service Academy athletic programs designed to advance concussion care research. Our clinical, research, and educational efforts are also closely coordinated with our sister Services through the TBI Advisory Committee, which consists of members from each Service as well as the Defense Health Agency.

Although most mild TBI care is appropriately delivered at the primary care level, the Air Force has specialized TBI clinics located at Joint Base-Elmendorf Richardson and the United States Air Force Academy. In addition, several premier referral centers are available for more complex cases to include the network of Intrepid Spirit Centers and the National Intrepid Center of Excellence for Psychological Health and Traumatic Brain Injury.

The Air Force is partnering across the force to better care for our Airmen and their families who have sustained Invisible Wounds. In 2016, the Under Secretary of the Air Force appointed a Special Assistant to coordinate Service-wide efforts to identify and resolve gaps in care for Airmen with Invisible Wounds. The Air Force Medical Service is a full partner in this effort, taking the lead on implementing 16 proposed solutions and supporting other directorates on another 11 which collectively span areas involving education and training, culture, process, policy, and care delivery. Additionally, we have established an Interim Medical Review Panel at the Under Secretary's request to ensure those currently going through the Integrated Disability Evaluation System for Invisible Wound conditions have received proper, evidence-based care. These panels began reviewing cases in January of this year and are in the process of compiling their 90-day observations and recommendations for further review and action. From the outset, this program is being pursued as a Total Force initiative, in recognition of the selfless service of our Reserve Component Airmen, and the injuries they have suffered alongside our active forces in the performance of their duties. Our collective Air Force efforts will engage with, and meet the needs of, our Airmen along the entire continuum of care.

Another initiative under this collective work is the Air Force's establishment of an Invisible Wounds Center of Excellence at Eglin Air Force Base, Florida, which was modeled after the DoD's Intrepid Spirit Satellite Clinic. Scheduled to open in 2018, the clinic will focus on those with PTSD, TBI, and associated chronic pain conditions and will provide a range of multidisciplinary diagnostic, treatment and rehabilitation capabilities tailored to individual patient's needs. Besides serving the needs of those Airmen and families in the Eglin area, the facility will serve as both a referral and telemedicine hub for the region and the entire Air Force.

While the Air Force Medical Service is a vital partner in supporting our Airmen, this is truly a "Team Sport" involving multiple Air Force, DoD, VA, and external partners to fully meet the needs of our Airmen and their families. We ensure our members receive extensive information on veteran health care benefits through the Transition Assistance Program that consists of individually-tailored briefings and career guidance. Seamless care for members with PTSD and TBI is delivered through the transition initiative which assigns counselors to Air Force members to make sure they receive timely follow-on appointments in the VA system once they are no longer in active duty status.

In tandem with this effort is the Air Force's proactive veteran transition support through the Interagency Care Coordination Committee. The committee enables the successful transition of service members and veterans who require complex care coordination between the DoD and VA through an integrated, interagency Community of Practice. Committee members have established DoD-VA interagency overarching guidance and ensure policies are congruent for delivering complex care, benefits, and services. The committee also strives to enable the use of a single, shared comprehensive plan for service members and veterans in need of complex care, benefits and services.

Many advantages will be realized from our effective treatment of PTSD and TBI. First and foremost, successfully treating these conditions eases the burden placed on our Airmen and their families, reducing distress and suffering, and improving resiliency and fitness. Second, effective management of these illnesses decreases the need for intensive support by units, commanders, supervisors and fellow Airmen, allowing these other individuals to devote greater focus to the readiness mission. Lastly, as affected Airmen recover, they themselves return to the fight, improving their sense of purpose and well-being and allowing them to contribute effectively to their unit's mission. These three results are synergistic, leading to positive improvements in the resiliency and readiness of Airmen with Invisible Wounds, their families, and their fellow Airmen.

Invisible Wounds affects lives and careers in many ways. We are therefore faithfully committed to providing the most effective prevention methods, research and treatment to support our Airmen with honor, dignity, and respect. I wish to thank the committee for its interest in this important topic, and for your ongoing dedication to the welfare of our Airmen, veterans, and their families.

Colonel Steven E. Pflanz

Col. Steven E. Pflanz serves as the Director of Psychological Health, Air Force Medical Support Agency, Falls Church, Va. He oversees Air Force mental health policy, plans and programs, interacts with Department of Defense partners, civilian research institutions, and units in the field to reduce suicides and optimize mental health care for Airmen.

Colonel Pflanz is a board-certified psychiatrist and rated flight surgeon who has served more than 22 years in the Air Force. He has previously served as the Chief of the Air Force Suicide Prevention Program, Chief of Air Force Physician Utilization, a squadron commander, Chief of the Medical Staff, and two assignments as a Mental Health Flight Commander. Additionally, he deployed to Afghanistan as commander of a combat and operational stress control detachment in 2012.

He has served as a school board member in the Randolph Field Independent School District, President of the Society of Uniformed Services Psychiatrists, and two-term President of the Academy of Organizational and Occupational Psychiatry.

He entered active duty in the Air Force after completing medical school in 1995.

EDUCATION
1990 Bachelor's Degree in Human Development and Family Studies, Cornell University, Ithaca, N.Y.
1990 Health Professions Officer Indoctrination Course, Lackland AFB, San Antonio, Texas
1994 Doctor of Medicine Degree, University of Rochester School of Medicine, Rochester, N.Y.
1995 Psychiatry Internship, University of Rochester School of Medicine, Rochester, N.Y.
1997 Aerospace Medicine Primary Course, USAF School of Aerospace Medicine, Wright-Patterson, AFB, Ohio
1998 Psychiatry Residency, San Antonio Uniformed Services Health Education Consortium, San Antonio, Texas
2002 Air Command and Staff College, by correspondence
2010 Air War College, by correspondence

ASSIGNMENTS
1. July 1995 – July 1998, Psychiatry Resident Physician, 59th Medical Wing, Lackland Air Force Base, Texas
2. July 1998 – June 2003, Mental Health Flight Commander, 90th Medical Operations Squadron, F.E. Warren AFB, Wyo.
3. July 2003 – August 2005, Mental Health Flight Commander, 305th Medical Operations Squadron, McGuire AFB, N.J.
4. August 2005 – August 2008, Chief of the Air Force Suicide Prevention Program and Senior Psychiatry Policy Analyst, Air Force Medical Operations Agency, Falls Church, Va.
5. August 2008 – July 2010, Commander, 579th Medical Operations Squadron, Bolling AFB, D.C.
6. July 2010 – August 2012, Chief of the Medical Staff, 90th Medical Group, F. E. Warren AFB, Wyo.
7. August 2012 – September 2016, Chief of Air Force Physician Utilization, Air Force Personnel Center, Randolph AFB, Texas
8. October 2016 – Present, Director of Psychological Health, Air Force Medical Support Agency, Falls Church, Va.

MAJOR AWARDS AND DECORATIONS
Bronze Star
Meritorious Service Medal (Five Oak Leaf Clusters)
Air Force Outstanding Unit Award (Three Oak Leaf Clusters)
National Defense Service Medal

Afghanistan Campaign Medal
Global War on Terrorism Expeditionary Medal
Global War on Terrorism Service Medal
Nuclear Deterrence Operations Service Medal (One Oak Leaf Cluster)
Air Force Expeditionary Service Ribbon
Air Force Longevity Service (Four Oak Leaf Clusters)
Air Force Training Ribbon
NATO International Security Assistance Force Medal

PROFESSIONAL CERTIFICATION
2000 American Board of Psychiatry & Neurology (most recent recertification in 2010)

PROFESSIONAL AFFILIATIONS
1. American Psychiatric Association – Fellow (Chair, Committee on Psychiatry in the Workplace, 2003-2006)
2. Society of Uniformed Services Psychiatrists – Immediate Past President 2016 to present (Previously held positions: President 2015-2016, Vice President 2014-2015, Treasurer 2013-2014)
3. American Psychiatric Association Foundation's Partnership for Workplace Mental Health's Partnership Advisory Council, 2006 to present
4. Academy of Organizational and Occupational Psychiatry – President 2006-2010, Vice President 2004-2006
5. Annual Meeting Program Chair 2002-2006
6. Suicide Prevention Action Network National Board of Directors, 2006-2009
7. Federal Government Suicide Prevention Committee, Chair 2006-2008
8. Wyoming State Suicide Prevention Task Force, 2001-2003

EFFECTIVE DATES OF PROMOTION
Captain May 22, 1994
Major May 22, 2000
Lieutenant Colonel May 22, 2006
Colonel May 22, 2012

(Current as of April 2017)

RECORD VERSION

STATEMENT BY
LIEUTENANT COLONEL (PROMOTABLE) CHRISTOPHER G. IVANY
ARMY DIRECTOR OF PSYCHOLOGICAL HEALTH
UNITED STATES ARMY MEDICAL COMMAND

BEFORE THE

HOUSE ARMED SERVICES COMMITTEE
MILITARY PERSONNEL SUBCOMMITTEE

FIRST SESSION, 115TH CONGRESS

ON POST-TRAUMATIC STRESS DISORDER AND TRAUMATIC BRAIN INJURY -
CLINICAL AND RESEARCH PROGRAM ASSESSMENT

APRIL 27, 2017

NOT FOR PUBLICATION UNTIL RELEASED BY THE
HOUSE COMMITTEE ON ARMED SERVICES

Chairman Coffman, Ranking Member Speier, and distinguished members of the subcommittee, thank you for this opportunity to provide a perspective on the treatment of Soldiers with behavioral health conditions, including Post Traumatic Stress Disorder, and Traumatic Brain Injury (TBI).

Over the past decade, I have witnessed the profound transformation of the Army's system for delivering behavioral health care to Soldiers and their Family Members impacted by conflicts around the world. I know of no other health care system in the nation that has improved behavioral health access, quality, and safety over a short period of time as extensively as Army Medicine. The Army committed to a multi-year transformation process to identify best practices in the field, incorporate emerging research findings, and standardize clinical operations across the enterprise. This approach has reduced variance between Army hospitals and improved the effectiveness of care. Army behavioral health providers are now positioned closer to the point of need, which reduces barriers to care. Our providers have new insights into the impact of their treatment through the use of one of the nation's leading methods for measurement-based care. While much work remains to be done, Soldiers are more ready to fight the nation's wars than they were several years ago.

Moving Care to the Point of Need

One of the core components of the Army's approach to enhancing behavioral health care delivery has been to eliminate barriers to care by moving teams of health care providers to locations that are more accessible to Soldiers and Family Members and developing working relationships with key stakeholders. For Soldiers, this approach is called Embedded Behavioral Health (EBH). Through the EBH program, Army Medicine aligns teams of behavioral health professionals with specific combat units. In most cases, EBH teams provide clinical care out of a small clinic located close to where Soldiers in that unit live and work. Informed by findings from Army researchers on stigma and barriers to care, EBH was pioneered at Fort Carson in 2009. EBH has been correlated with improved access to and continuity of care, a reduction in stigma to receiving behavioral health care, and fewer high risk behaviors, such as suicide attempts. The Army has adopted this model of care for all combat units and now operates 62 EBH teams with a total of over 450 behavioral health providers. Leaders in Army combat units have embraced this model of care and partnered with EBH teams to support Soldiers at risk for adverse events and improve the readiness of their units.

In a similar way, Army Medicine identified the need to more effectively provide access to behavioral health care for our Soldiers' children. We partnered with leaders in the civilian community, including the Universities of Maryland and South Carolina, to develop a School Behavioral Health program within Department of Defense schools located on Army installations. Through this effort, Army Medicine has placed behavioral health providers into small clinics in 60 schools and has plans to expand to 40 more in the next two years. School Behavioral Health providers offer convenient access to care and readily partner with school personnel, such as counselors, teachers and principals, to ensure that treatment is tailored to each patient's and enhances the readiness of the Soldier by decreasing the amount of time away from the unit for their child's appointment.

Embedded Behavioral Health and School Behavioral Healthcare are two examples of the innovative and wide-ranging improvements Army Medicine has implemented to better deliver behavioral health care. Soldiers and their Families now engage in outpatient care over twice as often as before changes were made. In 2007, Army beneficiaries participated in approximately 900,000 behavioral health visits. In 2016, that number grew to over two million. As more Soldiers have engaged in outpatient treatment, the need for inpatient care has decreased. Soldiers spent 67,000 fewer days in inpatient behavioral health facilities in 2016 than they did in 2012, which may indicate that behavioral health conditions are being treated before progressing to the point that inpatient care is required.

Measurement-Based Care

In the midst of transforming its behavioral health system of care, the Army recognized the need to measure the true effect of the care being provided to its beneficiaries. Unlike other areas of medicine, which easily lend themselves to objective outcome measures, such as blood pressure readings or laboratory results, behavioral health care is inherently subjective. To better ascertain the impact of behavioral health treatment, the Army developed one of the nation's leading platforms for measuring patient-centered outcome measures in behavioral health care.

The Behavioral Health Data Portal (BHDP) is an enterprise-wide web-application that enables standardized behavioral health assessments and outcome tracking in behavioral health clinics. Use of BHDP allows for real-time graphing of outcomes measures for clinical care, consolidation of data from multiple sources into one clinician dashboard, and aggregation of data for meaningful program evaluation. It was recently described in the Harvard Business Review as a leading practice for its ability to help providers personalize their treatment approaches to each patient.

The Army initiated BHDP in April 2012 and has since implemented it in all Army outpatient clinics, including virtual behavioral health. BHDP is expanding to include Intensive Outpatient Programs, Child and Family behavioral health, Family Advocacy, and Traumatic Brain Injury clinics. BHDP is now used in over 60,000 behavioral health encounters every month with over 2.2 million surveys collected to date. Each survey contains objective treatment outcome data that enables clinicians to better tailor treatment plans for each patient. BHDP has been endorsed as a best practice by the Assistant Secretary of Defense for Health Affairs and is being implemented across each Service. Finally, Army Medicine is working with Defense Health Agency leaders to include the core elements of BHDP into the new electronic health record.

The State of Treatment for Soldiers with Traumatic Brain Injury (TBI)

Since 2000, more than 357,000 Service members worldwide had a first time TBI diagnosis, of which approximately 58.5% (208,000) were U.S. Army Soldiers. The vast majority (approximately 85%) of those injuries were diagnosed in garrison non-deployed settings. However, due to the nature of combat operations, our Soldiers still have a higher likelihood of sustaining a TBI while deployed. Currently, there are no true diagnostic measures for concussion (also known as mild TBI) and no therapeutic treatments specific to TBI. For these reasons, the Army has invested in advancing the state-of-the-science and clinical care, while simultaneously using event-driven protocols to protect Soldiers from potentially concussive events. Army Medicine achieves this through a comprehensive program consisting of five essential elements: (1) a mandatory education component; (2) one world-wide standard of care; (3) an expansive garrison clinical care program; (4) baseline neurocognitive testing of deploying Soldiers, and (5) a gap-driven research program.

To complement medical and research efforts, Army Medicine leverages policy to enhance knowledge and standardize management of TBI. One aspect of the policy targets education and training for non-medical Soldiers, and focuses on leadership actions that will protect Soldiers after a potentially concussive event. A second Army policy effort targets the medical community by creating one world-wide standard of care through standardized evaluations and the use of jointly developed algorithms and clinical tools. Clinically, the Army also built an expansive garrison care capability, which is inclusive of 47 validated TBI programs. Additionally, the Army supports the joint force as the manager of the pre-deployment computerized neurocognitive testing program.

Providing optimized treatment is a priority of Army Medicine, however in the case of TBI, our efforts cannot and will not stop there. In 2017 and beyond, the strategic aims of the Army TBI program will be to enhance care, increase the impact of TBI research, and continue to generate a force trained to optimize TBI management.

Translating Research into Policy

The Army has been a leader in behavioral health research and continuously uses findings to inform behavioral health care policy and improve clinical programs. Army research studies that have been published in leading medical journals over the last 10 years include studies of factors influencing barriers to care, natural disease progression, effectiveness and utilization of clinical tools, and studies of the overlap in physical and behavioral health concerns following traumatic brain injury during deployment. Army Medicine has developed and refined policies as a direct result of this research. In particular, guidance to Army health care providers on the assessment and treatment of PTSD has evolved as new insights have emerged. Research has also informed other key areas, such as Army and DoD programs to reduce stigma and improve access, Combat and Operational Stress Control doctrine and training, and BH services delivered in primary care clinics.

The Army's ability to optimize care for Soldiers who have experienced Traumatic Brain Injuries also depends on a sharp understanding of the state-of-the-science. In FY16 alone, the Medical Research and Materiel Command invested $78M towards gap-driven research which includes projects targeting various capabilities including an objective diagnosis of mild TBI, a triage capability for the combat environment, and development of individualized rehabilitation plans. The Army will continue to maintain a strong link between its researchers and clinicians to ensure Soldiers and their Family Members receive the best available care.

Conclusion

Senior Army leaders recognize the direct link between behavioral health care and readiness and remain fully committed to further improving the treatment provided to Soldiers and their Family Members. The enhancements and innovations achieved by Army Medicine could not have been accomplished through the civilian health care system. The Army has tailored its behavioral health care system to the specific needs of Soldiers and their Family Members and is overcoming barriers to care, such as distance and stigma. While major changes have been made and significant progress has been realized, more remains to be done.

The most problematic barrier to continued improvements in behavioral health care is the maintenance of a stable hiring environment for civilians. The large majority of professionals working in behavioral health clinics are government civilians. Approximately 15% of our staff turns over each year. The Army depends on a consistent hiring process to ensure that a sufficient number of providers are available to deliver evidence based care.

We are committed to continuing to improve the health and readiness of our Soldiers and their Family Members. We look forward to continue to work with Congress in this effort. I want to thank my partners in the DoD, the VA, my colleagues on today's panel, and Congress for your continued support.

LTC Christopher Ivany, MD

Chris Ivany was born in Madison, WI and attended Providence College where he majored in Biology and earned his commission into the United States Army through ROTC in 1997. Chris then attended medical school at the University of Texas, Health Science Center in San Antonio, graduating with his M.D in 2001. He completed his internship and residency in Psychiatry at Walter Reed Army Medical Center in Washington, D.C., where he served as the Chief Resident in 2004-2005. He also completed a fellowship in Child and Adolescent Psychiatry at Tripler Army Medical Center in Honolulu, HI in 2007.

Chris has held several positions throughout his career. At Ft. Hood, TX he served as the 4th Infantry Division Psychiatrist and deployed to Baghdad in support of Operation Iraqi Freedom 07-09. At Ft. Carson, CO, he served as the Chief of the Department of Behavioral Health at Evans Army Community Hospital from 2010 to 2012. While there, he led the team that developed the Embedded Behavioral Health model of outpatient care for Soldiers, which has now become the standard across the Army.

LTC Ivany has served as the Chief of the Behavioral Health Division at the Army Office of the Surgeon General and as the Army Director of Psychological Health since April 2013.

Chris has several publications in national peer-reviewed journals. He has several professional recognitions and military awards, including the Bronze Star.

STATEMENT OF

CAPTAIN THOMAS M. JOHNSON, MC, USN

SITE DIRECTOR, INTREPID SPIRIT CONCUSSION RECOVERY CENTER

NAVAL HOSPITAL CAMP LEJEUNE

BEFORE THE

SUBCOMMITTEE ON MILITARY PERSONNEL

OF THE

HOUSE ARMED SERVICES COMMITTEE

SUBJECT:

POST-TRAUMATIC STRESS DISORDER AND TRAUMATIC BRAIN INJURY – CLINICAL AND RESEARCH PROGRAM ASSESSMENT

APRIL 27, 2017

Introduction

Chairman Coffman, Ranking Member Speier, distinguished Members of the subcommittee, thank you for providing me with the opportunity to share my perspectives as the director of the Intrepid Spirit Concussion Recovery Clinic (Intrepid Spirit) at Naval Hospital Camp Lejeune. We are responsible for the diagnosis and treatment of beneficiaries who have sustained a traumatic brain injury. In addition, I look forward to the opportunity to discuss potential process improvements and promising research in support of these injuries. It is a privilege to be entrusted with the care of service members and their families, and one that I and my colleagues at Camp Lejeune and across Navy Medicine take very seriously.

Background

Marine Corps Base Camp Lejeune is in a sparsely populated, rural part of eastern North Carolina. The base consists of 156,000 acres of open fields, forests, and coastline and is an ideal place for Marines to get the training they need to fight and win on the battlefield. This remoteness also means that it is in an area with limited civilian medical and research assets. The nearest major medical center is approximately a two hour drive away.

Traumatic Brain Injury, or TBI, has been described as the signature injury of the wars of Iraq and Afghanistan. Since 2000, more than 360,000 service members have been diagnosed with a TBI. A TBI is defined as a force applied to the head that temporarily or permanently disrupts brain function. The huge spectrum of severity of injury is often divided into mild, moderate, and severe. Approximately 20 percent of TBIs are classified as moderate to severe. The remaining 80 percent are classified as mild TBIs, otherwise known as concussions. Individuals may or may not have a brief period of loss of consciousness (less than 30 minutes); alteration of consciousness and memory for less than 24 hours; and a minimal alteration in neurological function as defined by the Glasgow Coma Score. Computerized Axial Tomography or CT scans, as well as other neuro-imaging modalities, typically show no evidence of abnormality in individuals who have sustained a mild TBI. Individuals who have sustained a mild TBI may only experience subtle changes in mood, memory, sleep and balance. There is currently no diagnostic tool that is sensitive and specific for mild TBI. The diagnosis is further confounded by the fact that the event causing the mild TBI often occurs as part of an intense training exercise, or in the chaos of battle and the fog of war.

As a result, the nonspecific symptoms described by the service members may be so subtle that only the service member and those who know him or her well realize that something is wrong. It can be unclear if the problem is due to mild TBI or to other commonly associated etiologies, such as post-traumatic stress (PTS), post-traumatic stress disorder (PTSD), migraine, sleep disorders, substance abuse, chronic pain, or a combination of some or all of the above. These warfighters have no visible sign of their injury but are often struggling to function at work, home, and in the community. Many times they are able to carry on from one deployment to the next, frequently minimizing injuries and occasionally self-medicating to get by – existing, but not really living life to the fullest. They and their families are the people we typically care for at Intrepid Spirit Camp Lejeune.

Caring for Service Members and Their Families

In response to the challenge of caring for these warfighters and their families in an area with scarce health care resources, Naval Hospital Camp Lejeune developed a comprehensive TBI recovery program in 2011 and the Fallen Heroes Fund gifted Camp Lejeune with a state of the art building in 2013. In addition to diagnosis and treatment, there is a research and educational component to the program, but the bulk of our work is clinical in nature. It is important to note that we care for Sailors, Marines, Soldiers, Airmen, and Coast Guardsmen. Our mission is to treat the physical, emotional, and spiritual injuries of service members and the families of service members who have sustained a brain injury. They may also have other conditions such as PTSD, chronic pain, polypharmacy and substance abuse issues that all contribute to their functional impairment. Irrespective of the exact mechanism of their brain injury, the goal is brain recovery.

When a service member who is stationed at or around Camp Lejeune enters our program they undergo a standardized, comprehensive evaluation by a multi-disciplinary care team that includes: a neurological examination; lab work; hearing; vision and vestibular testing; behavioral health; speech; language; and cognitive evaluations. Additional assessment, such as imaging or consultation with other specialties, is done as clinically indicated. The service members are also offered the opportunity to meet with pastoral care to assess the moral injuries they may have sustained. We also give the service members the opportunity to "tell their story" in an open-ended interview with representatives of their treatment team. They can invite anyone they wish to join them. They are asked three questions: What happened to you? What problems are you having? What can we do to help?

The treatment plan, developed in partnership with the service member, is tailored to meet his or her individual needs and goals. The implementation includes regular treatment team meetings with the service member to review clinical progress and make adjustments to the treatment program. We treat the service members as warrior athletes, with the expectation that they will return to full duty upon completion of their time at Intrepid Spirit. This expectation is based in part on the concept of neuroplasticity, or the brain's ability to form new connections in order to compensate for injury or changes in the environment. We have learned from the wars in Iraq and

Afghanistan that there is far more potential for neuroplasticity in young, previously healthy individuals than was formerly recognized.

We employ state of the art pharmacology, behavioral health treatments, and rehabilitation to treat service members while they are at Intrepid Spirit. We also employ a great deal of complementary and integrative treatment modalities, such as: acupuncture; alpha stimulation; audio visual entrainment; yoga; biofeedback; art therapy; meditation; and other modalities in an effort to take advantage of neuroplasticity to help heal the brain. Another benefit of complementary and integrative medicine is that it may provide an alternative to medication. Service members are typically hesitant about taking a medication, but are very receptive to complementary and alternative medicine. We rarely use opioids in our treatment.

When the service member and the treatment team determine that they have reached the maximum benefit from the program, which is usually after about 8 to 12 weeks of treatment, they are either returned to full duty or referred for medical evaluation for fitness for duty. To date, we have treated over 2,300 service members stationed at or near Camp Lejeune and greater than 90 percent who complete the program return to full duty from the standpoint of their TBI, although some may be medically retired for other reasons.

Our success has resulted in a demand for our services from active duty members who are not at Camp Lejeune. In response to this demand, about a year ago we added another product line, modeled in part on the program at the National Intrepid Center of Excellence (NICoE) at the Walter Reed National Military Medical Center (WRNMMC). We call this program "Return To Forces." It is a shorter, more intensive program that consists of a one-week standard evaluation track and a five-week standard evaluation and treatment track. This compressed treatment time allows service members to be sent by their commands on temporary duty to Camp Lejeune and receive intensive treatment and then return to their commands so they are ready to get back into the fight.

To date, Return To Forces has treated over 80 service members in this program, with all of them going back to full duty. Many of the participants are from special operations commands and potentially have had several TBIs, as well as other injuries associated with many kinetic deployments over their career. They know they are injured, but their command's operational tempos are so high and they are so committed to the mission, that they did not take time to seek medical care for themselves. Their feedback about the Return To Forces program is frank, and insightful. They frequently mention complementary and integrative therapies as the services they found most beneficial during their time at Intrepid Spirit. We realize that this small group of talented, highly trained individuals is bearing a disproportionately large burden of fighting in the current conflicts, and our focus remains ensuring this population of elite warrior athletes have access to state of the art care they need and deserve. While the data on what works in these multi-disciplinary approaches are limited, we have been collecting information across Navy Medicine and partnering with the other Services, to identify improvements to treatment.

The collocation of providers in the Intrepid Spirit facility contributes to our success. Because the treatment team members are co-located with one another, they are able to share information about the service members they are treating and address issues within minutes with their colleagues. The Intrepid Spirit is an integrated practice unit that provides a unique mission critical capability of caring for service members who have sustained a TBI and the comorbidities associated with TBI, especially those that are combat-related.

Research and Collaborations

The Intrepid Spirit is uniquely situated to make significant contributions to TBI research. It has clinical and research assets that are collocated with the service members. The result is that the Intrepid Spirit has become a forum where clinicians, researchers, and warfighters can meet and share ideas, identify needs and gaps in knowledge and develop concepts that grow into research protocols that generate actionable information that actually helps the service members and their families. These endeavors are only possible through our partnerships with many top tier institutions. We are part of a network of Concussion Recovery Centers that include NICoE, at the WRNMMC, as well as other Intrepid Spirits across the Military Health System at Fort Belvoir, Fort Campbell, Fort Hood, Joint Base Lewis-McChord, Fort Bragg and Camp Pendleton. We regularly communicate best practices and lessons learned. We also receive support in the form of staffing and best practices/clinical recommendations from NICoE and the Defense and Veterans Brain Injury Center to help us in our clinical, educational, and research efforts.

We are working with our colleagues in the MHS and academia to identify gaps in knowledge so we can develop and execute protocols that address these gaps. We can then take what we have learned from research and apply it at the deck plate to improve care for services members and their families. We are partnering with institutions to include: East Carolina University; University of California Irvine; Syracuse Veterans Administration Medical Center; University of Pittsburgh Medical Center; Wayne State University; Princeton University; and University of Pennsylvania. These efforts are important to improve collaboration, break down silos, and minimize the impact of distance inasmuch as these academic centers of excellence can bring their tremendous intellectual firepower on the problems facing warfighters by helping us study the unique populations at places like Camp Lejeune. For example, we have training evolutions that include heavy weapons and breeching exercises that occur at predictable times and places, which to some degree replicate a combat environment. These exercises are just one example of a tremendous opportunity for partnerships between military and academia to study and better understand the mechanisms that cause TBI, as well how to best diagnose and treat it.

We have submitted protocols or have ongoing studies on various topics that include identifying clinical and MRI markers that predict outcome in service members who have sustained a TBI, identification of biomarkers associated with TBI, and the efficacy of various complementary and integrative treatment modalities. Future efforts could include long term longitudinal studies of the late effects of TBI and better understanding the relationship, if any, between TBI and neurodegenerative diseases such as Alzheimer's and Parkinson's disease, Chronic Traumatic Encephalopathy (CTE) and other diseases. Another area that merits further study is what role, if any, gender, plays in TBI – an important question as women play an increasingly prominent role in the Armed Forces.

In my view, prevention remains the best treatment for a TBI, so conjunction with our clinical and research efforts, we sustain a robust education component. This element includes presentations, briefs, and exhibits at various local meetings and events across the installation emphasizing the importance of safety and the use of protective equipment.

Moving Forward

We are encouraged, but not satisfied with the progress we have made in the care of service members who have sustained a TBI at Intrepid Spirit through the use of a holistic, integrated, interdisciplinary treatment model that is tailored to meet the needs of warfighters and their families. It is particularly gratifying to be focused on treatment modalities that minimize the need to use medications, especially narcotics. We continue to see the demand for our services and remain committed to our mission of caring for our injured service members and furthering our research efforts.

Every day, as we work with service members who have sustained a TBI, we are reminded of the urgency and the importance of our mission. On behalf of the staff at Naval Hospital Camp Lejeune, I would like to say we are grateful to the committee for your strong support of our efforts. We are blessed to have the chance to work hard at something that is so important and so rewarding. I am honored to have represented the men and women at Camp Lejeune, and all across Navy Medicine who work to deliver heath care anytime, anywhere.

Capt. Thomas Johnson, M.D., U.S. Navy
DVBIC Site Director

Capt. Tom Johnson is a native of Winona, Minn. He graduated with honors from Haverford College in 1985. He attended medical school at the University of Minnesota on a Navy Health Professions Scholarship. Upon graduating medical school in 1989, he came on active duty as a lieutenant. He interned at Portsmouth Naval Medical Center and then went on for additional training in undersea medicine. He served as a diving medical officer (DMO) for Submarine Squadron 14, Holy Loch, Scotland, from 1990 to 1992. He then did his residency in neurology at the National Naval Medical Center in Bethesda, Md., where he was awarded the John Hallenbeck award for outstanding resident. He went on to serve as a neurologist at Naval Hospital Camp Pendleton. In 1997 he was the DMO for the Cooperation Afloat Readiness and Training exercise conducted by the U.S. Navy with various other nations in Southeast Asia. Upon completion of the exercise he served as a neurologist at Naval Medical Center San Diego until 2002. He then went on to serve as a DMO at the Navy Experimental Diving Unit in Panama City Beach, Fla., where he was the principal investigator for the development of repetitive decompression tables for the Mk 16 MOD 1 underwater breathing apparatus. He was then assigned to Naval Medical Center Portsmouth from 2002 to 2006, during which time he served as a neurologist, as well as the specialty leader for Navy neurology community. He was then assigned temporary duty with the Marine Corps Center for Lessons Learned and deployed to Iraq to evaluate the care provided to service members with possible traumatic brain injury. He then served as a neurologist at Naval Hospital Camp Lejeune from 2006 to 2010. He then worked as a neurologist at the National Intrepid Center of Excellence from 2010-2011. He is currently at Camp Lejeune and is serving as the director of the Marine and Sailor Concussion Recovery Center.

Johnson is board certified in neurology, as well as undersea and hyperbaric medicine. He is also certified in acupuncture therapy. In addition, he has earned a diploma from the Naval War College. He has published a number of papers on traumatic brain injury, as well as a book on the psychological and social aspects of military conflict. His personal awards include: Meritorious Service Medal (2), Navy Commendation Medal, Navy Achievement Medal (3), Iraq Campaign Medal, and Sea Service Ribbon, and various other service and unit awards.

WITNESS RESPONSES TO QUESTIONS ASKED DURING THE HEARING

April 27, 2017

Captain COLSTON. The Department of Defense (DOD) is working to inform veterans and those discharged from the military of the brain tissue repository (BTR). Brain Injury Awareness month, supported by connected health efforts (e.g., internet, apps) and outreach events, advertises the crucial need for brain tissue donations to this repository. Service members can declare their desire to donate to a brain repository after death through a will or power of attorney. If no such documents exist, next-of-kin may also make a determination regarding donation. Donations will remain voluntary: ethical considerations forbid compelling the donation of brain tissue. DOD is also partnering with the Organ Procurement Organizations (OPOs) to establish a Memorandum of Understanding and Institutional Review Board approvals to obtain such specimens, since OPOs can reach out to individuals interested in brain donation. DOD plans similar outreach for the 15-year longitudinal study participants.   [See page 11.]

$$===$$

QUESTIONS SUBMITTED BY MEMBERS POST HEARING

APRIL 27, 2017

$$===$$

Mr. COFFMAN. As we know, traumatic brain injury (TBI) is a significant health issue that affects service members and veterans during times of both peace and war. In addition, there is growing evidence that TBI is associated with a variety of short- and long-term adverse health outcomes that may include the acceleration of the onset of brain disorders that may result in dementia and other disorders that affect memory, movement and mood.

Given this emerging link between mild, moderate and severe TBI and dementia, what initiatives are being undertaken by the Department and service surgeons general to advance research? How might the Department and services use public-private partnerships to advance their research, particularly as it relates to the link between TBI and dementia?

Captain COLSTON. The Department of Defense (DOD) recognizes the importance of following Service members diagnosed with Traumatic Brain Injury (TBI) for an extended period in order to define risk factors associated with the delayed onset of dementia or chronic traumatic encephalopathy. DOD currently conducts and supports multiple clinical research studies to diagnose TBI earlier and to better understand the progression of TBI symptoms. The Department also collaborates with several private and academic groups. Of the many research initiatives supported or conducted by DOD, three are of note. The first is the congressionally-mandated 15-year longitudinal study exploring the natural history of TBI. The study intends to improve our understanding of TBI through neurobehavioral, neurocognitive, neuro-imaging, blood specimen, sensory, and motor data from Service members and veterans injured since October 2001. It will document long-term outcomes and identify long-term, chronic effects of TBI. The second, one of several large-scale studies researching the relationship between TBI and neurodegenerative conditions, is the Chronic Effects of Neurotrauma Consortium, a DOD and VA collaboration exploring the long-term effects of mild TBI. The third, the DOD-sponsored National Collegiate Athletic Association Grand Challenge, targets collegiate athletes—including those at the military service academies—to ascertain the sequelae from concussion. DOD has played a key role in developing and supporting the Federal Interagency Traumatic Brain Injury Registry, which allows for data sharing across the entire TBI research community and for collaboration among research programs in the DOD, NIH, and academia. Additional DOD research includes efforts to better understand chronic traumatic encephalopathy (CTE). Two recent studies are noteworthy. One study examined postmortem brain specimens from eight military cases with chronic and acute blast exposure: this study found a distinct and previously undocumented pattern of brain scarring that could account for aspects of the behavioral symptoms of CTE. Beyond the results of these 8 brains, the repository includes approximately 80 samples and continues to accumulate more over time. The other study sought a premorbid test for CTE: this study, which used positron emission tomography (PET) scans, represents an important step toward identifying CTE in living Service members thought to be at risk.

Mr. COFFMAN. The medical-scientific literature indicates there is a paucity of data for women affected by brain injuries particularly in the armed services. Although there are clear historical reasons, thinking into the future, how is DOD making an effort to accumulate more data on female service members as related to issues of brain injuries?

Captain COLSTON. Given that sixteen percent of Service members are women, the Department of Defense (DOD) is working to accumulate more data on female Service members diagnosed with Traumatic Brain Injury (TBI). DOD has recently published on, and continues to investigate, gender differences in TBI. DOD is supporting several longitudinal studies designed to determine gender differences for the risk for TBI, differential clinical effects of TBI, intersex differences in symptom reporting, and differences in short- and long-term outcomes between sexes. Two of the largest studies are the congressionally-mandated 15-year longitudinal study and the Improve Understanding of Medical and Psychological Needs in Veterans and Service Members (IMAP) study. The 15-year study explores the natural history of TBI. The IMAP study investigates health care, mental health care, and the rehabilitation needs of female Service members after they complete inpatient treatment in DOD, the Department of Veterans Affairs, or both. It focuses on the needs of concussed female Service members, as well as on the health and behavioral needs of disabled Service members' caregivers, who are primarily women. The DOD-sponsored National Collegiate Athletic Association Grand Challenge Partnership and the Concussion Assessment, Research and Education Consortium also address gender differences.

Mr. COFFMAN. As we know, traumatic brain injury (TBI) is a significant health issue that affects service members and veterans during times of both peace and war. In addition, there is growing evidence that TBI is associated with a variety of short- and long-term adverse health outcomes that may include the acceleration of the onset of brain disorders that may result in dementia and other disorders that affect memory, movement and mood.

Given this emerging link between mild, moderate and severe TBI and dementia, what initiatives are being undertaken by the Department and service surgeons general to advance research? How might the Department and services use public-private partnerships to advance their research, particularly as it relates to the link between TBI and dementia?

Colonel PFLANZ. The Department of Defense has multiple ongoing initiatives to advance research into our understanding of TBI. Specifically, the ongoing, congressionally mandated 15-year longitudinal study is intended to increase our understanding and awareness of both short and long-term outcomes of TBI. This would include cognitive and behavioral changes that would be expected to occur in TBI-related dementia or chronic traumatic encephalopathy (CTE). The Chronic Effects of Neurotrauma Consortium (CENC) is a public-private, multi-center collaborative effort between DOD, VA, civilian academic institutions, and private research entities. The CENC mission is to foster research to better understand the long-term neurodegenerative outcomes following TBI in Service members and to find effective treatments. In addition, CENC aims to find ways to identify the Service members most susceptible to these adverse long-term outcomes. The DOD has also partnered with the National Collegiate Athletic Association (NCAA) in sponsoring the NCAA-DOD Grand Alliance. This $30 million project is intended to research and prevent concussions by investigating sport-related mild TBI (mTBI). The United States Air Force Academy and the sister Service academies are all participating sites for this ongoing research. Finally, DOD has been involved in the development and support of the Federal Interagency Traumatic Brain Injury Registry (FITBIR). This system is intended to foster sharing of data amongst those performing TBI research, including entities within DOD, other governmental agencies such as NIH, and civilian research centers.

Mr. COFFMAN. The medical-scientific literature indicates there is a paucity of data for women affected by brain injuries particularly in the armed services. Although there are clear historical reasons, thinking into the future, how is DOD making an effort to accumulate more data on female service members as related to issues of brain injuries?

Colonel PFLANZ. The ongoing, congressionally mandated 15-year longitudinal study of the natural history of TBI will allow meaningful comparisons between males and females exposed to TBI. In addition, the Improved Understanding of Medical and Psychological Needs in Veterans and Service members with Chronic TBI (IMAP Study) is another DOD and VA collaborative effort supported by the Services. Among other goals, this study is investigating the unique needs of female service members in terms of health care, mental health, and rehabilitation following TBI exposure.

Mr. COFFMAN. As we know, traumatic brain injury (TBI) is a significant health issue that affects service members and veterans during times of both peace and war. In addition, there is growing evidence that TBI is associated with a variety of short- and long-term adverse health outcomes that may include the acceleration of the onset of brain disorders that may result in dementia and other disorders that affect memory, movement and mood.

Given this emerging link between mild, moderate and severe TBI and dementia, what initiatives are being undertaken by the Department and service surgeons general to advance research? How might the Department and services use public-private partnerships to advance their research, particularly as it relates to the link between TBI and dementia?

Colonel IVANY. As the scientific evidence emerges on potential associations between TBI and dementia or other disorders which may affect memory, movement and mood, the Department of Defense (DOD) and Surgeons General seek answers through a research portfolio cultivated to evaluate the spectrum of injuries. The DOD achieves this by grooming a research strategy including focal areas such as understanding the neuropathophysiology (brain damage at the cellular level) in living and deceased models, identifying assessment and diagnostic techniques that correlate with structural brain changes, developing treatments to slow or reverse the progression of disease, and monitoring the natural progression of TBI. Importantly, the DOD's current Combat Casualty Care-Neurotrauma Research Portfolio includes 104 open studies ($483M), effectively covering the spectrum of TBI by severity of injury (mild to severe), location in the injury/care continuum (point of injury, rehabilitation, or longitudinal study), and technology readiness level (time until it is a viable product). This DOD strategy, in combination with active program management, ensures a diversified, yet gap-driven, portfolio which is most likely to deliver solutions relevant to Service Members with TBI. Moreover, the DOD recognizes the importance of interdepartmental coordination and public-private partnerships in order to successfully advance understanding of TBI and the state of the science. One DOD supported effort looking at the natural progression of TBI is the Chronic Effects of Neurotrauma Consortium (CENC). The CENC is a joint DOD and Department of Veterans Affairs (VA) effort addressing the long-term consequences of mild TBI in Veteran, Active Duty, Reserve, and National Guard populations. It is part of a larger collaboration stemming from Executive Order 13625, which initiated the National Research Action Plan (NRAP) for Improving Access to Mental Health Services for Veterans, Service Members, and Families. Additionally, the DOD portfolio includes other longitudinal studies that seek unique but complimentary results in military relevant populations. The Department expects the CENC, National Collegiate Athletic Association (NCAA)-DOD Grand Alliance (Concussion Assessment, Research and Education Consortium), and the DOD/VA 15 year longitudinal study of TBI (including a neurological/neurobehavioral clinical data, blood specimens, and psychosocial impacts) collectively will inform the natural progression and long-term effects of TBI in sports, military, and civilian populations. For optimal outcomes from the research investments, the DOD supports public-private partnerships within the TBI portfolio. One example is the TBI Endpoints Development (TED) study, which in coordination with the National Institutes of Health (NIH), leverages datasets containing thousands of TBI subjects to harmonize and curate data into a large meta-dataset. The project seeks to validate this dataset and enter into FDA qualification processes to become acceptable "standard measures" for clinical trials. The DOD strategy also supports the NRAP requirement to place all federally funded study data into the Federal Interagency Traumatic Brain Injury Registry (FITBIR), a secure, centralized informatics system developed to accelerate analysis. As of 30 APR 2017, the FITBIR maintains data from 60 studies include over 1.5 million records from 42,500 subjects.

Mr. COFFMAN. The medical-scientific literature indicates there is a paucity of data for women affected by brain injuries particularly in the armed services. Although there are clear historical reasons, thinking into the future, how is DOD making an effort to accumulate more data on female service members as related to issues of brain injuries?

Colonel IVANY. The Army and Department of Defense (DOD) recognize there is a limited amount of scientific literature specific to female Service Members affected by brain injuries. Historically military-related mild TBI (mTBI) studies did not include high numbers of women because of the relatively low prevalence of the injury to women in combat. Recognizing the increasing role of women across the range of military operations, and increased exposure to combat situations, the DOD has made a concerted effort to evaluate potential gender differences in incidence, symptoms, and outcomes after Combat and Non-Combat-Related mTBI. The Congressionally mandated 15 year longitudinal study of TBI, required on Section 721 of the FY 2007 NDAA, is already producing results specific to gender difference which should help inform clinical practice and future study design. The NCAA–DOD Grand Alliance (Concussion Assessment, Research and Education (CARE) Consortium), as well as a parallel study of non-NCAA Service Academy Cadets, seek enrollment of all women at the Service Academies, and will surely add to the body of literature. However, other studies seeking enrollment of women have faced continued challenges due to a low prevalence. The DOD effort to mitigate that limitation is leveraging data to look at the gender differences in healthcare utilization, and provide insight into TBI-related comorbidities, long-term consequences, and health care costs specific to women. Additionally, the DOD funds a number of studies that have set out to examine how gender impacts TBI outcome in Service Members or Veterans.

Mr. COFFMAN. As we know, traumatic brain injury (TBI) is a significant health issue that affects service members and veterans during times of both peace and war. In addition, there is growing evidence that TBI is associated with a variety of short- and long-term adverse health outcomes that may include the acceleration of the onset of brain disorders that may result in dementia and other disorders that affect memory, movement and mood.

Given this emerging link between mild, moderate and severe TBI and dementia, what initiatives are being undertaken by the Department and service surgeons general to advance research? How might the Department and services use public-private partnerships to advance their research, particularly as it relates to the link between TBI and dementia?

Captain JOHNSON. 1. The Intrepid Spirit Camp Lejeune, in partnership with Princeton University and Wayne State University are in the early phases of "A Prospective Study of the Effects of Repetitive Low Level Blast Exposure (RLLBE) on Fitness for Duty in SOCOM Warriors." Follow on efforts include the development of validated baseline testing tailored for individual warfighters that can be repeated after subsequently sustaining a TBI. This baseline testing would be used to determine what effects the exposure had on their performance, how long their recovery was, and when they were fit enough to return to duty. Additionally, the development of individualized baseline testing will allow providers to detect subtle changes in cognitive function throughout their life. Partnering these types of tools with clinical history contributes exponentially to a longitudinal study on the long term effects of TBI. Due to the nature and frequency of exposures, the Special Operations community would serve as the initial community that this may prove best suited.

2. The Surgeon General of the Navy has made partnerships one of his strategic priorities for Navy Medicine—Readiness, Health and Partnerships. As part of our initiative towards expanding and strengthening our partnerships to maximize readiness and health, we see significant potential for public-private partnerships as it relates to the advancement of research in TBI and dementia. In our pursuit to partner with academic, public, and private institutions, we are strategically assessing the landscape for future opportunities, removing barriers, and remaining vigilant that our partnerships are in alignment with our objectives. Intellectual sharing through partnerships can be a more cost effective and yet very impactful way to advance research.

Mr. COFFMAN. The medical-scientific literature indicates there is a paucity of data for women affected by brain injuries particularly in the armed services. Although there are clear historical reasons, thinking into the future, how is DOD making an effort to accumulate more data on female service members as related to issues of brain injuries?

Captain JOHNSON. It is my understanding that the Department of Defense is pursuing a number of longitudinal studies to gain a greater understanding of the risk profile, long-term effects, clinical differences, and outcomes for female service members impacted by TBI. Specifically, the Intrepid Spirit Camp Lejeune has presented at a national meeting on TBI in female service members. In addition, we are in the process of finalizing the publication of a retrospective study of approximately 300 service members, four of which are women, seen at Intrepid Spirit Camp Lejeune who had a reported history of TBI due to blast exposure. It is my observation that a shared data base between the Intrepid Spirit Center Camp Lejeune and other military treatment facilities would significantly increase the data collection on women impacted by brain injuries in the Armed Forces. For this reason, the Intrepid Spirit Camp Lejeune is establishing the final parameters under which a Memorandum of Understanding (MOU) could effectively operate a shared database with the National Intrepid Center of Excellence (NICoE).

––––––––

QUESTIONS SUBMITTED BY MS. TSONGAS

Ms. TSONGAS. What are the current screening mechanisms that the services use to identify post-traumatic stress disorder (PTSD) for warfighters returning from deployment? What screening or monitoring measures are taken with service members who have suffered from PTSD before they are approved for a future deployment?

Captain COLSTON. The Department of Defense (DOD) screens Service members for symptoms of Post-traumatic Stress Disorder (PTSD) at multiple points within the deployment life cycle, including annual, pre-deployment, and post-deployment health assessments. Service members deployed in connection with a contingency operation are assessed for PTSD and depression symptoms, suicide and violence risk, and substance use disorders using person-to-person interviews at four different periods before and after deployment. These interviews, conducted by trained health care providers, expand upon self-reported survey responses and include a review of health records. Service members are then referred for follow-up evaluation and treatment, as needed. In accordance with DOD policy, health care providers notify a Service member's Commander regarding concerns (e.g., risk of harm to self or others, mission impairment). Service members are not cleared for subsequent deployments unless they are free of deployment-limiting mental health conditions.

Ms. TSONGAS. How are the services screening for PTSD in service members as a result of non-combat deployment related causes—such as military sexual trauma that may not have been previously reported, for example? Specifically, please address how the FY15 NDAA requirement for annual mental health screening of service members has been implemented and what is covered in the screening.

Captain COLSTON. The Department of Defense (DOD) leverages a Primary Care Medical Home model, using an evidence-based screening instrument, to screen Service members for Post-traumatic Stress Disorder (PTSD). The Post-Traumatic Stress Checklist screens for trauma at multiple points regardless of deployment status. Screening is conducted for all new patients, existing patients annually, and any patients for whom it is clinically necessary. Patients with PTSD who receive ongoing mental health treatment are screened periodically until the end of their treatment. During intake for all mental health appointments, in accordance with health care accreditation standards, providers ask Service members a number of questions related to whether they have experienced trauma. DOD complies with the National Defense Authorization Act for Fiscal Year 2015. As part of annual periodic health assessment, Service members receive annual mental health screening. This assessment includes the use of evidence-based screening instruments that produce a self-report of depression symptoms, posttraumatic stress, alcohol misuse, and overall functioning. The annual assessment includes a follow-up interview with a trained health care provider to further assess identified symptoms, review medical documentation, and provide referrals for applicable treatment and evaluation.

Ms. TSONGAS. What requirements exist for mental health screening as service members leave active duty to ensure that PTSD and other mental health issues are identified during service and there is a warm handoff to the VA?

Captain COLSTON. During military separation, Service members must complete a separation health assessment that includes a review of medical history, medical concerns, and current health status. This assessment may be completed at a Department of Defense (DOD) or Department of Veterans Affairs (VA) facility—each entity shares results with the other. Service members currently receiving mental health care are automatically enrolled in the inTransition program during separation from the military. Service members can elect to opt out if they desire. The inTransition program supports a warm hand-off between the DOD and the VA for Service members who are in treatment for psychological health conditions by enhancing coordination between referring and gaining providers. Since the launch of the automatic enrollment requirement in April 2014, the inTransition program has completed 50,314 assessments in support of care transitions.

Ms. TSONGAS. We've heard in recent years of the development of new technologies that use physiological measurements to predict and help address the onset of PTSD episodes. What is the current research portfolio of technologies for the screening or monitoring of PTSD? Do the services see the measurement and use of physiological indicators as a way to provide even more comprehensive care to service members suffering from PTSD? What are the limitations in currently existing technologies?

Captain COLSTON. Efforts to predict or treat Post-traumatic Stress Disorder (PTSD) using physiological measures are in incipient stages. Investigations regarding the possible utility and functionality of biosensors are underway. Biosensors have the potential to aid screening, monitoring, and treatment of many psychological health conditions. The Department of Defense (DOD) is currently studying biosensors that look and feel like Band-Aids, "Fitbits," "Smartwatches," and other wearable technologies. These tools take physiological measurements and link to smartphones that collect data. While these innovative biosensors are not yet effective in clinical applications for PTSD treatment, they will likely be a part of PTSD management in the future. Studies continue to establish efficacy and then effectiveness in the field. Currently, DOD relies on evidence-based screening tools for the assessment and diagnosis of PTSD. For instance, the Post Traumatic Stress Checklist (PCL) is a series of questions that a patient answers and a provider scores. Providers integrate screening results with other clinical information to determine if patients meet criteria for PTSD. Since 2013, DOD has used a software platform and computer technology to create an electronic database, the Behavioral Health Data Portal, where patients' PCL responses are stored for providers to monitor. There are no predictive or diagnostic technologies beyond the research stage in DOD's current portfolio; several promising endeavors, however, are in progress. These include studies on Heart Rate Variability, attention bias biomarkers, brain imaging, and voice analysis. DOD is working to integrate technology into clinical care and apply technology to prevention efforts. Mobile applications for self-care tools that supplement treatment for Service members and veterans suffering from PTSD have been developed for use across the Services, DOD, and the Department of Veterans Affairs. Examples of these apps include PTSD Coach, PE Coach, and Dream EZ. Studies on the PTSD Coach indicated both high rates of perceived helpfulness and acceptability and also a reduction in some PTSD symptoms when combined with clinical treatment. While the measurement and use of physiological indicators (i.e., data that these apps help to collect) have not yet been incorporated into clinical care, substantial interest exists and research is underway to do so in the future. One challenge in developing technology to advance psychological health screening and treatment in DOD is privacy. Most applications use the internet to operate. It is difficult to interact digitally across the internet without attending to privacy issues. Additionally, technologies that support psychological health screening and treatment are new, so we are still learning how they can best aid Service members with PTSD. Finally, our understanding of the safety and effectiveness of the use of technology to support PTSD screening or treatment over time is limited. This is a challenge that merits further research.

————

QUESTIONS SUBMITTED BY MR. KNIGHT

Mr. KNIGHT. I am aware that Tinker Air Force base is currently conducting clinical trials on magnetic EEG/EKG-guided resonance therapy. Can you elaborate on the clinical trials and their results thus far? Are there any plans in the Department of Defense to expand these trials? Also, has Tinker AFB conducted clinical trials using repetitive transcranial magnetic stimulation (rTMS)?

Colonel PFLANZ. One study is underway on magnetic EEG/EKG-guided resonance therapy at Tinker AFB. The study is in its early stages, having completed the intervention with eight subjects so far; it is too early to draw any substantive conclusions. We are not aware of any plans for the Department of Defense to expand these trials. Tinker AFB has not conducted any clinical trials using repetitive transcranial magnetic stimulation (rTMS).

9 781983 964763